ANALYZING THE ISSUES

CRITICAL PERSPECTIVES ON SOCIAL JUSTICE

Edited by Jennifer Peters

Enslow Publishing

101 W. 23rd Street
Suite 240
New York, NY 10011
USA

enslow.com

Published in 2018 by Enslow Publishing, LLC
101 W. 23rd Street, Suite 240, New York, NY 10011

Library of Congress Cataloging-in-Publication Data

Names: Peters, Jennifer, editor.
Title: Critical perspectives on social justice / edited by Jennifer Peters.
Description: New York : Enslow Publishing, [2018] | Series: Analyzing the issues | Audience: Grades 7-12. | Includes bibliographical references and index.
Identifiers: LCCN 2017015486 | ISBN 9780766091658 (library bound) | ISBN 9780766095632 (paperback)
Subjects: LCSH: Social justice—Juvenile literature.
Classification: LCC HM671 .C758 2018 | DDC 303.3/72—dc23
LC record available at https://lccn.loc.gov/2017015486

Printed in China

To Our Readers: We have done our best to make sure all website addresses in this book were active and appropriate when we went to press. However, the author and the publisher have no control over and assume no liability for the material available on those websites or on any websites they may link to. Any comments or suggestions can be sent by email to customerservice@enslow.com.

Photo Credits: Cover The Washington Post/Getty Images; cover and interior pages graphic elements Thaiview/Shutterstock.com (cover top, pp. 1, 4–5), gbreezy/Shutterstock.com (magnifying glass), Ghornstern/Shutterstock.com (additional interior pages).

CONTENTS

INTRODUCTION 4

CHAPTER 1

WHAT THE EXPERTS SAY 6

CHAPTER 2

WHAT THE GOVERNMENT
AND POLITICIANS SAY.................................... 46

CHAPTER 3

WHAT THE COURTS SAY 65

CHAPTER 4

WHAT ADVOCACY
ORGANIZATIONS SAY 132

CHAPTER 5

WHAT THE MEDIA SAY 162

CHAPTER 6

WHAT ORDINARY CITIZENS SAY............. 181

CONCLUSION 212

BIBLIOGRAPHY.. 214
CHAPTER NOTES.. 217
GLOSSARY 226
FOR MORE INFORMATION.................................. 227
INDEX 228
ABOUT THE EDITOR.. 231

INTRODUCTION

From the fight for racial equality in the 1960s and the push for gender equality in the 1970s to the refugee crisis and the Black Lives Matter movement in 2016, matters of social justice have been a part of everyday life in America for decades—even centuries. When the pilgrims fled to the New World in search of religious freedom, they were technically seeking social justice—the freedom to worship as they saw fit without being discriminated against based on their religion. And the Native Americans they first encountered in the future United States eventually had to fight for social justice of their own—the right to be treated as citizens of a country that they had lived in for years before the Europeans arrived.

Social justice is defined as the equal distribution of wealth, opportunity, and privilege. To simplify it, social justice is achieved when people who are different—whether that's different genders, races, religions, sexual orientations, cultural backgrounds, economic classes—are treated the same. It means that men and women are paid the same for doing the same job, that black and white men and women are treated the same when confronted by law enforcement, and that Muslims and Christians are allowed to practice their religions freely and without persecution.

While this sounds like a very good thing, there are also many people who believe that "social justice" is part of what they consider "politically correct" or "PC" culture and that most people claiming to fight for social justice are actually trying to "police" the ways we speak and think or want to unfairly offer handouts to people who don't deserve them. Why is there such a difference of opinion on the importance of social justice? Some people simply think that America is already equal and that people are all given the same opportunities and treated the same. Others are opposed to social justice out of fear—fear that if others are treated the way they are now, they will have to be treated worse for it to balance out. Still others simply don't know that there are some people who are still treated unequally because of their differences, either because they've never experienced it or because they don't personally know anyone who has.

As you read over the articles in this book, you'll discover not only viewpoints expressing the importance of social justice and the ways in which the fight for equality has shaped our history, but also the opposing side, in which people who feel any continued fight for social justice is unnecessary. By looking at how experts, academics, the American court system, and everyday people view social justice, you'll get a 360-degree view of the issue, and you'll have a chance to decide for yourself how much social justice matters—both to America as a whole and in your everyday life.

CHAPTER 1

WHAT THE EXPERTS SAY

Experts and academics who study social justice issues focus on every aspect of social inequality, from race and economics, to religion, to the effects of global warming. Many social justice issues, you'll learn, are made up of more than one basic issue, and forms of inequality often have impacts on other issues of injustice. For example, as you'll read in an article by Kathryn Green, climate change can be discussed in terms of social justice as it generally impacts those who are already economically vulnerable. You'll also learn how some forms of inequality can lead to further issues of social injustice, as Keith Matthee SC discusses in his article about the cycle of violence in the fight for social justice.

"INEQUALITY: THE RHETORIC AND REALITY," BY JAMES A. DORN, FROM THE FOUNDATION FOR ECONOMIC EDUCATION, JUNE 22, 2015

The publication of Thomas Piketty's bestseller *Capital in the Twenty-First Century* has led to widespread attention on the rising gap between rich and poor, and to populist calls for government to redistribute income and wealth.

Purveyors of that rhetoric, however, overlook the reality that when the state plays a major role in leveling differences in income and wealth, economic freedom is eroded. The problem is, economic freedom is the true engine of progress for all people.

Income and wealth are created in the process of discovering and expanding new markets. Innovation and entrepreneurship extend the range of choices open to people. And yet not everyone is equal in their contribution to this process. There are differences among people in their abilities, motivations, and entrepreneurial talent, not to mention their life circumstances.

Those differences are the basis of comparative advantage and the gains from voluntary exchanges on private free markets. Both rich and poor gain from free markets; trade is not a zero- or negative-sum game.

Attacking the rich, as if they are guilty of some crime, and calling for state action to bring about a "fairer" distribution of income and wealth leads to an ethos of envy — certainly not one that supports the foundations of abundance: private property, personal responsibility, and freedom.

In an open market system, people who create new products and services prosper, as do consumers. Entrepreneurs create wealth and choices. The role of the state should be to safeguard rights to property and let markets flourish. When state power trumps free markets, choices are narrowed and opportunities for wealth creation are lost.

Throughout history, governments have discriminated against the rich, ultimately harming the poor. Central planning should have taught us that replacing private entrepreneurs with government bureaucrats merely politicizes economic life and concentrates power; it does not widen choices or increase income mobility.

Peter Bauer, a pioneer in development economics, recognized early on that "in a modern open society, the accumulation of wealth, especially great wealth, normally results from activities which extend the choices of others."

Government has the power to coerce, but private entrepreneurs must persuade consumers to buy their products and convince investors to support their vision. The process of "creative destruction," as described by Joseph Schumpeter, means that dynastic wealth is often short-lived.

Bauer preferred to use the term "economic differences" rather than "economic inequality." He did so because he thought the former would convey more meaning than the latter. The rhetoric of inequality fosters populism and even extremism in the quest for egalitarian outcomes. In contrast, speaking of differences recognizes reality and reminds us that "differences in readiness to utilize economic opportunities — willingness to innovate, to assume risk, to organize — are highly significant in explaining economic differences in open societies."

What interested Bauer was how to increase the range of choices open to people, not how to use government to reduce differences in income and wealth. As Bauer reminded us,

> Political power implies the ability of rulers forcibly to restrict the choices open to those they rule. Enforced reduction or removal of economic differences emerging from voluntary arrangements extends and intensifies the inequality of coercive power.

Equal freedom under a just rule of law and limited government doesn't mean that everyone will be equal in their endowments, motivations, or aptitudes. Disallowing those differences, however, destroys the driving force behind wealth creation and poverty reduction. There is no better example than China.

Under Mao Zedong, private entrepreneurs were outlawed, as was private property, which is the foundation of free markets. Slogans such as "Strike hard against the slightest sign of private ownership" allowed little room for improving the plight of the poor. The establishment of communes during the "Great Leap Forward" (1958–1961) and the centralization of economic decision making led to the Great Famine, ended civil society, and imposed an iron fence around individualism while following a policy of forced egalitarianism.

In contrast, China's paramount leader Deng Xiaoping allowed the resurgence of markets and opened China to the outside world. Now the largest trading nation in the world, China has demonstrated that economic liberalization is the best cure for broadening people's choices and has allowed hundreds of millions of people to lift themselves out of poverty.

Deng's slogan "To get rich is glorious" is in stark contrast to Mao's leveling schemes. In 1978, and as recently as 2002, there were no Chinese billionaires; today there are 220. That change would not have been possible without the development of China as a trading nation.

There are now 536 billionaires in the United States and growing animosity against the "1 percent" — especially by those who were harmed by the Great Recession. Nevertheless, polls have shown that most Americans think economic growth is far more important than capping the incomes of the very rich or narrowing the income gap. Only 3 percent of those polled by CBS and the *New York Times* in January thought that economic inequality was the primary problem facing the nation. Most Americans are more concerned with income mobility — that is, moving up the income ladder — then with penalizing success.

Regardless, some politicians will use inflammatory rhetoric to make differences between rich and poor the focus of their campaigns in the presidential election season. In doing so, they should recognize the risks that government intervention in the creation and distribution of income and wealth pose for a free society and for all-around prosperity.

Government policies can widen the gap between rich and poor through corporate welfare, through unconventional monetary policy that penalizes savers while pumping up asset prices, and through minimum wage laws and other legislation that price low-skilled workers out of the market and thus impede income mobility.

A positive program designed to foster economic growth — and leave people free to choose — by lowering marginal tax rates on labor and capital, reducing costly regulations, slowing the growth of government, and normalizing monetary policy would be the best medicine to benefit both rich and poor.

1. One of the author's arguments is that governments are often biased against the rich, and because they choose to help the poor instead of the rich, they are inadvertently hurting the poor. Based on this article, do you think that the author is right? If so, how can helping the rich promote social justice for the poor?

2. The author says that government focus on income inequality actually helps to widen the wealth gap because of the way the governments create new rules and regulations. Does the government have an obligation to help the poor as a matter of social and economic justice?

"REPORT: PRIVATIZATION DRIVES INEQUALITY," BY SHEILA KENNEDY, FROM INEQUALITY.ORG, OCTOBER 4, 2016

A NEW STUDY OUTLINES THE NEGATIVE IMPACT OF CONTRACTING PUBLIC SERVICES TO PRIVATE COMPANIES.

I am one of those tiresome academics who has repeatedly criticized so-called privatization of government functions. I say "so-called" because what Americans call privatization is no such thing. Actual privatization would require government to sell off or otherwise abandon a particular activity, and let the private sector handle it, much like Margaret Thatcher selling England's steel mills to private-sector interests.

What we call privatization is more accurately described as contracting out: Government retains both responsibility for a service and the obligation to fund it, but delivers the service through a third-party surrogate, either for-profit or not-for-profit.

There are certainly instances where choosing such a surrogate makes sense. Unfortunately, we Americans tend to embrace fads in government as elsewhere. So rather than engaging in analyses of risk and reward, too many public entities have accepted the argument that nongovernmental actors will do a better job, no matter how essentially governmental the function.

Research results strongly suggest otherwise. And now, with the publication of an in-depth report, *In the Public Interest* has illustrated the pernicious effects much contracting has had on equality. The report centers on five ways in which contracting exacerbates inequality:

"User-funded contracting." Public budgets have tightened all across the country, largely due to the American public's unwillingness to pay taxes to support the services we continue to demand. As a result, some jurisdictions are allowing contractors to charge fees to end-users to subsidize or completely fund an outsourced service.

This is increasingly happening in areas where citizens have little to no political voice. In private probation, for example, offenders are expected to pay for everything from their own drug testing to the costs of ankle-bracelets, despite the fact that as a group they lack the resources to do so.

Rising rates. Residents of places that have privatized critical public services such as water or transit have experienced steep increases in their rates. Some of these increases can be attributed to the profit motive, but in other jurisdictions—like my own—the increases mask desperate, clandestine efforts to shift the costs of public infrastructure from taxpayers to ratepayers. In Indianapolis, the city sold the water company, which—thanks to deferred maintenance needs—had a negative value of several billion dollars. Citizens Energy, which purchased it, then "adjusted" its payments in lieu of taxes, or PILOT obligation, upward. That allowed the city to float bonds, repayable from the artificially increased PILOT, and use the proceeds to pave deteriorated streets. The result was to shift the costs of infrastructure repair from general tax revenues to utility ratepayers. It would be hard to think of a more regressive strategy.

Cutting the social safety net. Programs like Medicaid and food assistance are often subjects of privatization experiments, and the report notes that the impact can be tragic. Contractors have increasingly taken over critical social services like child foster care services, welfare, the distribution of food assistance, Medicaid, and child support services. But as the report details, the complex social problems faced by families and children who utilize these services are difficult, if not impossible, to address using a privatization model, and many social services contracts have financial incentives that inadvertently perpetuate cycles of poverty and divert money from critical programs to corporate profits.

Indiana, again, provides an example. Then-Governor Mitch Daniels attempted to outsource welfare intake; as a result, many recipients were denied benefits to which they were clearly entitled, and others endured long waits and confusing processes. The results were so negative that the effort was discontinued, but the ensuing lawsuits cost the state millions of dollars that might otherwise have provided needed services.

A race to the bottom for workers. One of the recurring criticisms of privatization has been that, when private companies take control of a public service, they often slash wages and benefits to cut costs, replacing stable, middle-class jobs with poverty-level jobs. The report confirms the criticism.

Similarly, the report underlines increasing recognition that privatizing schools, especially, **increases socioeconomic and racial segregation.** As the text notes, introducing private interests into things like schools and public parks can—and often does—radically impact access for certain groups.

The report is a sobering reminder that there is a critical difference between *procurement*—government purchases of such things as street paving or computers—and *contracting out* delivery of core governmental responsibilities. As it concludes: "Weakening democratic control over public goods and services increases economic, political, and racial inequality."

1. The author argues that privatizing certain public services—like schools—increases the inequality between classes and races, because already-marginalized groups can't afford the same things as wealthier or more privileged classes. After

reading this article, do you agree that privatization hurts, or can it be used to help increase equality?

2. Through privatization, the author says, people who are entitled to certain forms of government assistance are denied because the private groups set different parameters. Do you think the government has a responsibility to help marginalized groups directly, or does it have the right to outsource that assistance, even if it means helping fewer people?

EXCERPT FROM "SOCIAL JUSTICE AND SOCIAL ORDER: BINDING MORALITIES ACROSS THE POLITICAL SPECTRUM," BY RONNIE JANOFF-BULMAN AND NATE C. CARNES, FROM PLOS, MARCH 31, 2016

MODEL OF MORAL MOTIVES (MMM)

There are two broad but distinct ways of being moral: engaging in positive, selfless behaviors or restraining negative, self-interested behaviors. These are motivationally distinct, for the former involves the need to establish new "good" motivations, whereas the latter involves inhibiting pre-existing "bad" motivations. In drawing this distinction, Janoff-Bulman, Sheikh and Hepp [1] labelled these two broad orientations prescriptive morality *(the shoulds)* and proscriptive morality (*the should nots*), and noted that they reflected differences between approach and avoidance applied to the moral domain. Keeping self-interest in check (e.g., restraining the temptation to lie or cheat) is clearly moral, but it is not the same as actually helping another—that is, not harming is not equivalent to helping. Proscriptive and prescriptive morality represent two distinct motivations: proscriptive morality relies on behavioral inhibition to restrict the "bad," whereas prescriptive morality involves behavioral activation to enable the "good."

In our recent effort to map the moral domain, we relied on this motivational distinction to generate discrete moral motives [2,3]. More specifically, we crossed proscriptive and prescriptive morality with the three primary domains of behavior studied by psychologists—the intrapersonal (self), the interpersonal (another), and the collective (group). As evident in Fig 1, the resulting six cells are: Self-Restraint, Industriousness, Not Harming, Helping/Fairness, Social Order, and Social Justice. In the first column are the self-focused moral motives. Here MMM identifies Self-Restraint (proscriptive) and Industriousness (prescriptive) as intrapersonal moral motives, involving moderation and attributes often associated with the "protestant ethic" respectively. Although these motives focus on the self, they involve distal benefits for group survival in countering wastefulness (i.e., via moderation) and contributing to the groups' resources and competencies (i.e., via hard work, persistence). Recent research by Hofmann and colleagues [4] on moral acts in everyday life provides support for the claim that such self-directed moral principles should be included in any comprehensive model of morality.

	Self (Personal)	Other (Interpersonal)	Group (Collective)
Proscriptive Morality	Self-Restraint	Not Harming	Social Order
Prescriptive Morality	Industriousness	Helping/Fairness	Social Justice

The center (interpersonal) column of MMM [2] refers to our interactions with specific, identifiable others, and the two cells—Not Harming and Helping/Fairness—reflect the prototypes of morality for both proscriptive and prescriptive regulation [5]. Not harming involves not only refraining from physically hurting another, but also inhibiting behaviors such as lying and stealing that would otherwise advantage the actor. Helping entails providing for the well-being of another; fairness, too, is a prescriptive moral motive in the interpersonal domain and involves giving others their due. The close relationship between helping and fairness are evident in their early integration in the phenomenon of reciprocal altruism.

All of morality ultimately involves the facilitation of group living and group survival, but the proximal behaviors need not focus specifically on the group, as evident from the preceding four cells of MMM. However, the third and final column of MMM focuses specifically on the collective and entails broad social regulation. As Tomasello and Vaish [6] write, the evolution of morality involves a two-step process: "...the first step is mutualistic collaboration and prosocially motivated interactions with specific individuals, and the second step is the more abstract, agent-neutral, norm-based morality of individuals who live in more large-scale cultural worlds full of impersonal and mutually known conventions, norms, and institutions" (p. 232).

There are two group moral motives in MMM: Social Order (proscriptive) and Social Justice (prescriptive). Most generally, Social Order is in the service of collective coordination, and is particularly responsive to dangers and threats to the group, whether physical threats to safety or psychological threats to identity. A Social Order morality emphasizes the importance of group conformity and strict adherence to behavioral norms; self-interest and individual self-expression are constrained in the service of the larger group's interests. Social Justice involves communal responsibility and activates collective efforts to advance the group's welfare. There is a particular focus on equality-based distributional justice. Most generally, a Social Order morality is oriented towards protecting the group, whereas a Social Justice morality is oriented towards providing for the group [2,7].

TWO GROUP MORALITIES

In this paper we focus on the two group moralities of MMM, for we believe they address a provocative issue raised by Moral Foundations Theory (MFT). More specifically, Haidt and colleagues [8–11] in the dominant model of morality to date (MFT), posit five moral foundations. There are two "individualizing" foundations—Harm/Care and Fairness/Reciprocity—where the individual is the focus of moral concern; these involve "individual-focused contractual approaches to society" (p. 369) [8]. In addition there are three "binding" foundations—Ingroup/Loyalty, Authority/Respect, and Purity/Sanctity—that bind people together; their focus of moral concern is the group [8].

Using MFT, Haidt and colleagues [8,12–14]) note that liberals emphasize the individualizing foundations, whereas conservatives rely on both the individualizing and binding foundations—that is, conservative morality is based in all five foundations, whereas liberal morality is based in only two. The provocative implication of these assertions is that liberals don't have a morality that is focused on the group; this is the provenance of only conservatives.

Yet the binding (i.e., group) moralities in MFT are all aspects of a Social Order morality; they are mechanisms in the service of a binding proscriptive moral regulation [2,3]. Haidt and colleagues overlook a prescriptive group morality—Social Justice. We contend their conclusion that only conservatives have a group morality is a consequence of failing to include a group morality that might represent liberal (versus conservative) moral motives.

It is important to address possible reactions claiming that Social Justice is really the same as Fairness/Reciprocity, which is included in MFT. Although they may be used interchangeably in everyday conversation, they are nevertheless distinct constructs [2,3 for a more detailed discussion]. Paralleling the important distinction between microjustice and macrojustice by Brickman, Folger, Goode, and Schul [15], fairness is based in considerations of another's deservingness and involves identifiable others whose inputs or attributes are assessed. In contrast, social justice is based in considerations of the distribution of resources across a group; it is deindividuating and focused on the group or, more specifically, others as categorical members of the group [16,17 for similar distinctions]. As in MMM, Fairness is appropriately regarded as an individualizing foundation in MFT, and considerable past research has found minimal liberal-conservative differences in this moral foundation. In contrast, we believe Social Justice is endorsed far more by liberals than conservatives.

It might also be argued that Social Justice is really the same as care, as represented by the Harm/Care foundation in MFT [18]. To some extent, from a sufficiently distal perspective, all of morality is about harm and care [5,19], yet individuated Care entails known, identifiable others and assessment of need, whereas Social Justice is about the form of a distribution across a group and its fit with equality concerns. Again, Social Justice is a binding, group-based morality, whereas Harm/Care is an individualizing morality endorsed by both liberals and conservatives.

Contrary to MFT, our claim is that there is a group-based morality for liberals, and that it is Social Justice. More specifically, we propose two distinct group moralities—Social Order and Social Justice, with the former positively associated with political liberalism and the latter with political conservatism. Liberals, in other words, do have a group morality; it simply hasn't been included in MFT, the dominant model of morality to date.

SELF-REGULATION VERSUS SOCIAL-REGULATION

What might account for the hypothesized positive associations between conservatism and Social Order and between liberalism and Social Justice? To answer this question, we can turn to differences in fundamental motivational orientation. Here we draw from past work to suggest that an avoidance motivation is dominant for conservatives, whereas an approach motivation is dominant for liberals. More specifically, past research has found that conservatives are more reactive to threat, display greater disgust sensitivity, have greater category restrictiveness, are more apt to be the product of restrictive parenting, focus on losses rather than gains and show a general negativity bias; in contrast, liberals exhibit greater openness to experience, engage in more exploratory behaviors, are more apt to be the product of egalitarian parenting, and focus on gains rather than losses [20–34]. Conservatives' greater avoidance orientation and liberals' greater approach orientation provide a basis for the proposed differences found in group morality, because Social Order is a proscriptive avoidance-based moral motive, whereas Social Justice is a prescriptive, approach-based moral motive.

The distinct motivational proclivities of liberals and conservatives may account for differences in the group moralities, but raise a different but related question. Given the expected differences in the binding group morality of liberals versus conservatives (i.e., Social Justice and Social Order), it seems important to consider why the moral differences are expected to arise in this domain and not the others (i.e., self or interpersonal). This expectation is consistent with the MFT finding of few differences in the individualizing foundations based on political ideology. How might we account for the expected differences in Social Justice and Social Order, but not the other four cells of MMM?

The self and interpersonal cells are guides for how we should act (or refrain from acting) with regard to ourselves and specific, identifiable others. They are about self-regulation—regulating individual behavior with regard to the self or another. The group moral motives are guides for how we should act with regard to the group, but more important, they are broadly about how collectives should be run and monitored. This is the domain of social regulation. In the case of self-regulation, the appropriate level of analysis is clearly the individual, and there is typically some "balance" within the individual. That is, regardless of political orientation, we rely on both proscriptive and prescriptive morality. A moral person would be high on both Self-Restraint and Industriousness, and on both Helping/Fairness and Not Harming. Even a motivational proclivity for one or the other would not preclude considerable reliance on the other. In fact, a strong over-reliance on one or the other form of moral regulation is likely to be maladaptive when we are dealing with self-regulation [35].

When it comes to self-regulation, we can rely on both systems for maximal flexibility, and greater morality in one system is likely to be associated with being more moral in the other. Yet when we are considering social regulation, the level of analysis is now the group or collective. Balance may still be desirable for societal adaptability, but now it is can be achieved across individuals as opposed to within individuals. More specifically, an effective way to maintain balance would be for some subpopulations to espouse one group-based morality and others to advocate the other group-based morality. In this way, society can rely on both systems (i.e., proscriptive and prescriptive—Social Order and Social Justice) for maximal adaptability.

[...]

GENERAL DISCUSSION

Although liberals and conservatives share a common morality in the intrapersonal and interpersonal domains, they diverge when it comes to group-based moral motives. Here conservatives emphasize Social Order, whereas liberals stress Societal Justice. Libertarians are low on both binding group moralities; it appears they believe societal decisions should be based on individual autonomy across the board rather than collective concerns. Conservatives' Social Order morality is reflected in tight societies, with their emphasis on strict norm adherence and relative intolerance of behavioral deviance. Liberals' Social Justice morality, in contrast, seems more closely associated with loose societies, with their emphasis on normative openness and their greater association with egalitarianism. Interestingly, societies that balance tightness and looseness appear to be those that experience the greatest success, as assessed by both economic outcomes and subjective well-being in the current research. Based on these findings, it is intriguing to entertain the possibility that societies with strong advocates on both sides of the political spectrum may succeed in part because of the balance afforded by their opposition.

Morality facilitates social living; it helps us live together in interdependent groups. This functional perspective suggests that distinct moral motives are likely to address different societal challenges. A group morality based in Social Order is likely to be particularly effective in response to threats that require coordinated actions, whereas a group morality based in Social Justice is likely to be particularly effective when cooperative efforts are called for to improve group welfare. Not surprisingly, then, in recent work we found that Social Justice is associated with trust of unknown others, which is required for cooperative efforts; in contrast, Social Order is associated with generalized distrust, and thus the need for strong leadership and loyalty (i.e., MFT binding foundations) in the service of conformity and order [49]. There are likely to be costs and benefits associated with either orientation alone. A Social Order orientation may minimize risks associated with free riding and social loafing, whereas a group morality based in Social Justice may minimize the lost opportunities apt to be associated with the transaction costs of Social Order.

Some recent work in political science has argued that political ideologies are in our DNA [23,50]. It seems questionable that such broad ideologies are genetic, but it is certainly possible that motivational differences that we suggest may underlie these ideologies—and are reflected in distinct group moralities—may have some basis in basic temperament and physiology. Work reviewed above on increased reactivity to threat by conservatives [20,28,32], for example, is suggestive of such a perspective. Yet the differences reflected in endorsement of Social Order versus Social Justice are surely apt to be the result of multiple factors involved in socialization and life experience. Thus, in our own research we found that restrictive parenting was positively associated with a grown child's Social Order orientation [26]. Such parenting focuses on proscriptions (should nots) and tries to control the child's behavior through strict limits, threats, and punishment. Lenient parenting, the opposite of restrictiveness, was not associated with Social Justice (and nurturant parenting was not associated with either group morality). However, leniency is unlikely to describe the openness that accounts for greater inclusion of others, a feature of Social Justice [2,3]. Greater acceptance of difference—and of others who are different—may underlie Social Justice and suggests the importance of life experience. It is not surprising, for example, that large cities, with their tremendous diversity, are generally politically liberal, and reported above, Social Justice is strongly correlated with liberalism. In 2012, 27 of the 30 most populous cities in the U.S. voted Democratic; even every one of Texas' major cities—Austin, Houston, Dallas, and San Antonio—all voted Democratic in the midst of a very Republican state [51]. There is certainly self-selection in terms of who chooses to live in an urban area, reflecting a pre-existing openness to broader experience, but it is also likely that the experience of living in a city has a further impact as well. In the end, it is likely that multiple factors, from temperament and personality to parents and other socializing agents (e.g., other family members, teachers, friends) to lived experiences, contribute to an individual's support for Social Order or Social Justice and political orientation more generally. In recognizing the benefits of balance in group moralities suggested by the current research, we were drawn to results of presidential elections in the United States. An interesting feature of these contests is just how close they are in every four-year cycle; that is, we have been struck by the marked balance in left-right voting in these national elections. In the past 50 years, averaged across elections since 1964 (i.e., 13 presidential elections), 51.76% of the percent of the popular vote has gone to the winning presidential candidate, and when we consider all presidential elections between 1828 and 2012 (47 elections), the average percent of the popular vote going to the winning candidate changes very slightly to 51.80% [52]. (The popular vote was not recorded prior to 1824, so the first nine presidential elections are not included. We have also not included the 1824 election, because John Quincy Adams won with 30.92% of the vote. If this election is included, the average percent popular vote from 1824 through 2012 is 51.36%.)

Partisans on one side of the political spectrum no doubt find it hard to believe there are so many people on the other side. Yet election cycle after election cycle, with very few exceptions, some sort of equilibrium seems to be operating in the electorate, with liberals and conservatives, Democrats and Republicans, voting in relatively equal numbers for the candidate of their choice. Rather than cause for consternation or concern, perhaps this pattern should be considered an implicit indicator of societal success.

Those of us with strong political views on one side or the other no doubt regard this view of adaptive balance as unpalatable. The nature of morality, including group morality (i.e., Social Order and Social Justice), is such that we regard our own convictions as absolute, objective and necessarily right [53]. We thus feel certain that a society based wholly on our own morality would surely be best. Yet the reality on the ground is that we maintain our own moral perspective at the same time that others are pushing for opposing positions [54], balancing our own views. It is this system of countervailing views that may be adaptive in the end.

No doubt the current political paralysis in the U.S. would lead to the opposite conclusion—that is, that the opposing group moralities are clearly maladaptive in a single political system. We would suggest, however, that this is attributable not to the group-based moralities per se, but to a two-party system bent on electoral success rather than societal success. Politics requires negotiation and compromise, conciliation and concessions on the path to middle ground. The group moralities are socially evolved orientations that contribute to group survival across varied historical and ecological circumstances. Perhaps we would all benefit from recognizing that our political positions are not only conflicting, but ultimately complementary when viewed from the grander perspective of long-term societal success.

1. The authors of the above article discuss how openness to other people and willingness to be inclusive are components of social justice, and that having more life experience could lead a person to be more interested in promoting and achieving social justice. What sort of experiences do you think could lead a person to being more interested in social justice issues? What experiences do you think would lead a person to feel less concerned about social justice?

2. Within the article, social justice is discussed in terms of its relation to "group morality," or the

idea that certain shared experiences and ideas will be used to regulate behavior. What are some social justice issues that you think stem from specific groups and not the community as a whole?

"WHY LIFE IS TOUGHER FOR SHORT MEN AND OVERWEIGHT WOMEN," BY TIMOTHY FRAYLING AND JESSICA TYRRELL, FROM *THE CONVERSATION* WITH THE PARTNERSHIP OF THE UNIVERSITY OF EXETER, MARCH 9, 2016

Are you a short man or an overweight woman? If so, you may have a slight disadvantage in life compared with taller men and thinner women.

Our latest study has found evidence that men who are shorter due to their genes have lower incomes, lower levels of education, and lowlier occupations than their taller counterparts. The effect of height on socioeconomic status was much weaker in women. In contrast, women who have a higher body mass index (BMI) due to their genes have lower standards of living and household incomes. Having a higher BMI didn't seem to have the same negative effect on men.

DON'T WE KNOW THIS ALREADY?

Why did we want to do this study? After all, didn't we know that height and BMI are associated with socioeconomic status? And you can't change your genes, so why is this study interesting?

It's true that we have known for a long time that being short is associated with poverty, almost certainly because poor nutrition in childhood stunts growth. But the relationship between fatness and poverty is more nuanced.

In the not too distant past being thin was associated with poverty, and being overweight with wealth because people with more money were able to eat more. However, in the past few generations, in developed countries, that association has reversed. As we have moved to a world where calorie-dense food is readily and cheaply available, and life has become more sedentary, lower standards of living are associated with higher BMIs. But in this study we wanted to answer questions about causality rather than associations, which is why we turned to genetics.

YOU CAN'T CHANGE YOUR GENES

Associations between genes and human traits are likely to be cause not consequence. We can make this statement because your genes don't change.

A disease can't change your DNA sequence, but your DNA sequence can influence your chances of developing a disease, growing more, or your vulnerability to obesity. Once your father's sperm has fertilised your mother's egg, you are stuck with those two copies of the human genome and with some exceptions, such as in cancer cells, those two DNA sequences change very little during our lifetimes.

The different environments we encounter, the lifestyle choices we make, and the diseases we develop do not change the DNA sequences we inherit from our parents – to be clear, we are not discussing epigenetics here, where the environment can change how genes activate and deactivate.

SHORTER MEN AND HEAVIER WOMEN ARE POORER

We used demographic and genetic data from 120,000 people (aged between 40 and 70) in the UK Biobank. The study used 400 genetic variants that are associated with height, and 70 associated with BMI, together with actual height and weight, to ask whether or not shorter stature or higher BMI could lead to lower chances in life – as measured by information the participants provided about their lives.

Having analysed the data, we found that men who were 7.5cm shorter, for no other reason than their genes, on average earned £1,500 a year less than their taller counterparts. Meanwhile, women who were 6.3kg heavier, for no other reason than their genes, on average earned £1,500 a year less than the lighter women of the same height.

It's important to note that these are estimates and averages – short men and heavier women can, and do, succeed in life. Instead, it shows that across the population overweight women and shorter men are, on average, slightly worse off.

WHAT ARE THE IMPLICATIONS?

We now need to understand the factors that lead people who are overweight or short to lower standards of living.

Is the link down to low self-esteem or depression, for example? Or is it more to do with discrimination?

In a world where we are obsessed with body image, are employers biased? And do we need to pay more attention to potential unconscious biases in order not to unfairly discriminate against people who are shorter (especially men) or overweight (especially women)?

More studies are needed using data from other birth cohorts – the UK Biobank is biased towards thinner people and wealthier people because they had to actively participate in a study about health and this bias may have affected the results (that is, made the associations slightly weaker).

The study was also limited to people born between 1935 and 1971 and so the effects may no longer exist in younger adults today. It will be interesting to study the effects in young adults – it may be that the higher levels of obesity would exacerbate the problem, or it may be that society is far more accepting of fatter people and that factors such as discrimination and social esteem, if they were key to this data, are less important in younger generations.

The study provides a much needed advance in understanding a classic chicken or egg problem. But something about having a higher BMI as a woman, and shorter height as a man, does lead to being worse off in life.

1. While men who are shorter and women who weigh more are not necessarily protected or marginalized classes the same way African Americans or deaf people are, do you think the

studies referenced in this articles show that there needs to be social justice for people of different appearances? Do shorter men and heavier women need the same sorts of protections since their appearance is affecting their opportunities and economic situations?

2. It's assumed that it's pretty easy to know if someone is being marginalized because of their race, gender, religion, or economic class, but what if a man is short and black, or a woman is obese and Muslim? Do you think those people are more vulnerable than people who are of average height and weight, even if they are of a marginalized group?

"BRING SOCIAL JUSTICE IN FROM THE COLD AS WE GET CLOSER TO A GLOBAL CLIMATE CHANGE DEAL," BY KATHRYN GREEN, FROM *THE CONVERSATION* WITH THE PARTNERSHIP OF THE UNIVERSITY OF SHEFFIELD, SEPTEMBER 24, 2014

The UN Climate Summit in New York brought together politics, business and civil society to build up momentum for major climate change talks in Paris next year. After the disappointments of the acrimonious Copenhagen meeting in 2009, there is now a chance for a global agreement on action against climate change. Low carbon development pledges and substantial financing of the Green Climate Fund are one side of the coin.

But climate justice is also about social justice, and leaders must address the demands and respect the needs of people most vulnerable and already suffering from the impacts of climate change. The world's poorest people are the worst affected by climate change and these groups were certainly represented in New York, but will they be listened to?

If it is to have a lasting impact, the Paris meeting must successfully integrate a "top-down" global agreement to restrict global warming to 2°C, together with a "bottom-up" strategy whereby countries set their own contributions to reduced emissions. However, this latter strategy must go beyond emissions and do more to ensure that action on climate change listens to the grassroots and prioritises the world's poorest and most vulnerable groups.

GRASSROOTS CONCERN

The summit looked promising for proponents of an inclusive, "bottom-up" strategy. Its key themes included forests, agriculture and resilience to climate change, all of which have a sizable body of evidence to show that placing people directly affected at centre stage is a critical opportunity for success. There was also a thematic session on Voices from the Climate Front Lines which gave a platform to children, women and indigenous people suffering the effects of climate change.

However, the outcomes don't match the hype. There were specific examples of progress: the president of Peru outlined a strategy for reducing emissions from deforestation and degradation that he said would put the country on a path to sustainability by reaching out to indigenous groups and securing a vast area of land under indigenous rights.

He won public support from both Germany and Norway, and France also pledged funds to help the poor cope with climate change, but the global commitment to social justice called for by the Rights and Resources Initiative and the World Resources Institute was largely missing.

The anticipated, voluntary New York declaration on forests was marred by Brazil's refusal to sign up, and the seven action statements released following the summit directly address local people's rights and roles just twice (and one of these requires action from indigenous civil society groups rather than national or international governments).

Similarly, the Global Agricultural Alliance aims to secure "climate smart" agriculture for 500m farmers by 2030. However, it was left to civil society organisations to release a joint statement prioritising making food systems socially just and protecting the poorest and most vulnerable in these efforts.

The recently published New Climate Economy report outlines a vision for "better growth, better climate," a win-win scenario that ties investment and innovation to poverty and hunger reduction. But while investment and innovation may be able to secure the 70% more calories they estimate humans will collectively require by 2050, it is unclear how it will address the political aspects of access to those calories, and whether such strategies can support the livelihoods and resilience of the poorest farmers.

CLIMATE JUSTICE, SOCIAL JUSTICE

Without putting social justice at the core of our thinking on climate action, we risk harming the most vulnerable groups of people. For example, environmental concerns have been used by big corporations and national governments to justify claiming land for themselves, a process known as green grabbing that threatens the well-being of groups dependent on natural resources. Perhaps, we can eventually find a way to put people on an equal footing with the green economy but, judging from developments in New York, we don't seem to be there yet.

Paris must be about much more than the pledges on emissions and the green economy that have dominated the headlines since the UN summit. It appears New York was yet another example of a big international climate forum recognising the importance of social justice (itself a big achievement) without actually clarifying how it will be built into objectives or commitments. People will remain on the agenda, but not quite centre stage.

1. The author argues that denying climate change and not working to slow it means putting already vulnerable populations at even more risk as natural resources become more scarce and more expensive. What are some communities you believe are at risk because of climate change?

"JUSTIFYING THE USE OF VIOLENCE TO FIGHT SOCIAL INJUSTICE IS A RECIPE FOR DISASTER," BY KEITH MATTHEE SC, FROM *THE CONVERSATION* WITH THE PARTNERSHIP OF STELLENBOSCH UNIVERSITY, OCTOBER 19, 2016

South Africa is reaping the bitter fruits of violence: both apartheid's and the African National Congress's armed struggle.

At his 1964 trial for treason Nelson Mandela set out the basis for the African National Congress's (ANC) decision to use violence to fight the violence of apartheid. At one stage he stated:

> This conclusion, My Lord, was not easily arrived at. It was when … all channels of peaceful protest had been barred to us, that the decision was made to embark on violent forms of struggle.

At round about the same time across the Atlantic Ocean in the US, Martin Luther King wrote:

> *It would be both cowardly and immoral for you patiently to accept injustice…. But as you continue your righteous protest … be sure that the means you employ are as pure as the end you seek. Never succumb to the temptation of becoming bitter. As you press on for justice, be sure to move with dignity and discipline, using love as your chief weapon. Let no man pull you so low that you hate him. Always avoid violence. If you sow the seeds of violence in your struggle, unborn generations will reap the whirlwind of social disintegration.*

South Africa's university campuses are burning as students protest, demanding "free, decolonised education." Those students using violence, inter alia, argue that justice demands the use of such violence and that in effect it is a form of self defence.

Should they heed Mandela, or King?

A VIOLENT SOCIETY

There is an all pervasive presence of violence and contempt for human life in South Africa. Nothing illustrates this more graphically than abortion statistics and the rape of children.

Extrapolating from King's words, it would be difficult not to conclude that the ANC's prescription for fighting apartheid was shortsighted. It also did not grasp King's insights about the inevitability of reaping what one sows when opting for violence.

Crucial to King's thinking was that violence has a life of its own. The ANC, for its part, believed that the consequences of the decision to use violence could be controlled and managed.

Even more fundamentally, the ANC failed to grasp or understand the full consequences of justifying the use of violence to achieve a "noble" end. One consequence of this is that it provided the generations that followed the justification to use whatever means necessary to achieve their "just" ends.

In the 1980s I was often a defence advocate in "necklace" murder trials. Necklacing involved forcing a tyre over the shoulders of a person accused of collaborating with the apartheid government. The tyre, doused in petrol, would then be set alight. Necklacing as a means to cast off oppression was, to paraphrase King, "the end in the making."

FEEDING THE TYRANT

The point King makes is that once one opts for violence as a strategy to fight injustice, the devastating consequences will prevail for a long time afterwards.

His point was that meeting violence with violence only serves to feed the tyrant. To apply King's challenge to South Africa, the aim should have been to starve the violence of the twin tyrant of the Nationalist Party (the party of apartheid) and white capital through militant non-violent civil disobedience.

Even when the ANC was unbanned in 1990 it refused to abandon the "armed struggle" until it achieved its ends, as Anthea Jeffery writes in her book People's War (page 462). In this way it continued to feed the tyrant of violence which diminished the value and dignity of all human life.

Thousands of people were murdered between 1990 and 1994, many by the forces of the Nationalist Party, but many also by a brutal fight for power leading up to the 1994 elections between *inter alia* the ANC, IFP, Pan Africanist Congress and Azanian People's Organisation.

And then in 1994 there was an attempt to preach reconciliation, love, tolerance and nonviolence. But, by then, morally speaking, the nation had been grievously damaged. It had been dehumanised by apartheid, and the use of violence to fight it. It had been established on the hatred central to the use of violence.

The evil of apartheid combined with the ANC's decision to fight violence with violence, and to use violence in its own internal conflicts, was a toxic cocktail. The results are still with us today.

This is evident in the violent turn the student protests have taken. A student recently stated on national television that the only option open for the protesters was to use violence, or to threaten the use of violence, until their demands were met.

TAKING THE HIGH ROAD

King's aim was to shame the racists, to stir their consciences. Fundamental to this was the belief that hatred and violence should be met with militant non-violent action. Crucially, this also meant being prepared to take the full consequences of such action. These consequences included imprisonment, beatings and even death.

If South African students were to embrace King, I have no doubt that those with economic power would be shamed and their consciences stirred. The overwhelming majority of ordinary South Africans also would come out in open support for the just cause of making tertiary education accessible to the poor and powerless.

South Africa's students could make a significant contribution to the nation's moral regeneration if they disavowed violence and took the high road espoused by King.

As a nation, we are still reaping the fruits of the violence of apartheid and the use of violence to fight it. South Africa's students can help the country break that cycle. And is it not central to the call of university students to say no to the status quo, in this case the use of violence, and to provide a new and better way?

A concluding thought by King is also cause for further reflection:

> *It (the nonviolent approach) does something to the hearts and souls of those committed to it. It gives them new self-respect.*

1. The author discusses how violence used to fight social injustice often leads to new forms of injustice. After reading the above article, do you think fighting social injustice through violence is ever helpful? Explain.

2. In this article, Nelson Mandela and Martin Luther King Jr. are discussed, as are their views on the use of violent protest in the fight for social justice. Mandela's South Africa was notoriously violent, while King's fight for civil rights in the US was at times violent, but was frequently more peaceful. From what you've read above and what you know of those civil rights movements in each country, do you think things would have turned out differently had the US civil rights battle been more violent? What about if the South African fight had been more peaceful?

"WHY INEQUALITY MATTERS – FOR THE RICH AND THE POOR," BY ALESSANDRA MEZZADRI, FROM *THE CONVERSATION* WITH THE PARTNERSHIP OF SOAS, UNIVERSITY OF LONDON, OCTOBER 2, 2015

In the last decade, there has been a renaissance in studies stressing the relevance of inequality worldwide, particularly in the aftermath of the 2008 global financial crisis. The loud cry of the Occupy movement gained worldwide attention in its denunciation of the increasing polarisation of incomes and assets in the hands of an infamous 1%.

Thomas Piketty's *Capital in the Twenty-first Century* has largely supported the claims of global social movements that capitalism is moulding a world for the few against the many. It is not a coincidence that the name of his book recalls Karl Marx's famous critique of political economy.

Since the 1950s, mainstream economic narratives have been obsessed with modelling the relationship between inequality and growth. They also deployed questionable indicators of inequality based on an "average" distribution (the Gini coefficient).

Piketty has broken this mould. His work has focused on the extremes of the distribution and on elite's capture since the origins of capitalism in western economies.

This enabled him to highlight what capitalism does best if left unchecked: namely, increasing returns to capital, rewarding and reproducing the creation of wealth. The book has been widely reviewed – favourably and unfavourably. Truth is, whatever one thinks about it, it returned inequality to the core of political economy debates on capitalism where it belongs.

ROOTS OF INEQUALITY

In many instances, the historical roots of intercountry inequalities lie in slavery and colonialism. This is too often overlooked by contemporary economic analyses whose timeline is generally quite narrow. The Jamaican government is currently reminding the UK that slavery can hardly be dismissed as a "thing of the past."

Intracountry and intercountry inequalities interplay in the world economy. The increasing polarisation of the income shares of capital and labour is embedded in an equally polarised global division of labour.

This counterpoises countries hosting the majority of the world's rich, led by the US, and those gathering the majority of the world's working poor – Asia, Africa and Latin America. In the post-colonial era, national capital has played its own role in processes of exploitation and dispossession against the working poor.

British-Indian writer Rana Dasgupta has illustrated how these processes unfolded in the making of Delhi as a modern metropolis. Intriguingly, he has done so in a book also called Capital—a portrait of Delhi in the 21st century.

Even emerging economies like India or China, which are experiencing "global convergence," are building their economic fortune on the shoulders of the working poor.

THE COST OF INEQUALITY

The human and social cost of highly unequal processes of capitalist development for low classes and for the working poor is substantial. This should be the primary reason for our interest in inequality.

The Marikana tragedy, which saw South African police firing on striking miners with live ammunition killing thirty-four, has indicated the violent nature of the struggles over resources and income shares. Piketty himself refers to the Marikana case to highlight the extreme consequences of fights over redistribution.

In Cambodia in 2014, workers were shot in the streets of Phnom Penh as they asked for an increase in their minimum wage. Inequality must be fought because it perpetuates social injustice.

Even those hardly moved by these arguments are increasingly aware of the challenges highly unequal distributions of income and wealth imply. Inequality was high on the agenda at the World Economic Forum 2015 in Davos, certainly not your average activists' network. This is because high levels of inequality have clear economic and social costs.

High inequality may undermine growth, as in South Africa. It can lead to violence and tensions, compelling the rich to live in gated communities, like in Brazil. In Buenos Aires, there were 90 gated communities in the 1990s. They became 285 by 2001, and 541 by 2008.

The proliferation of borders, fences and walls, not only in urban spaces, is gaining momentum across the world, even in developed countries, leading to increasingly segregated livelihoods. In the end, also the rich may not want to live like this.

WHAT TO DO ABOUT IT?

This is hardly an easy question to answer. Economics studies, even bestsellers like Piketty's, still tell us little about who is more likely to bear the brunt of inequality. This is a crucial issue as inequality is a "horizontal," "group phenomenon" experienced collectively.

And income and wealth – material inequality – may only represent the final outcome of far more rooted structures of oppression.

Ultimately, inequality is experienced on the basis of class, gender, race, caste or geographical provenance. In South Africa, one cannot understand inequality without addressing the legacy of apartheid. In India, one cannot decouple inequality from colonialism and caste. In the US, inequality is linked to racial discrimination. In Europe, it is increasingly linked to migration, as many undocumented migrant workers are subjected to "slavery-like" working conditions.

The fight against inequality must be fought on many fronts. It is a fight worth fighting. As highlighted in all books of the Capital "trilogy" mentioned here, from Marx to Piketty and Dasgupta, inequality is a key functioning mechanism of capitalism. It must be addressed as a matter of social justice.

Furthermore, it may also soon become both economically unviable and socially undesirable for the few to exclude the many. As the few reinforce fences and gates, the many may be really becoming too many, particularly across the developing world. They may even start demanding their share.

1. Economic inequality is a form of social injustice that affects people around the world, regardless of race, gender, or religion. But the author discusses how economic inequality is often rooted in other forms of inequality, like slavery and colonialism. Based on the article above, do you think economic inequality is rooted in other forms of inequality, or do other forms of injustice grow out of economic inequality?

2. The author points out examples in which economic inequality has led to violent outcomes. After having read the previous article about violent protests, as well as this article, do you think violence will always be an outcome of injustice?

CHAPTER 2

WHAT THE GOVERNMENT AND POLITICIANS SAY

Politicians have long disagreed on matters of social justice. From the fight to end slavery in the 1800s to the fight for civil rights in the 1960s to the modern-day fight for equal access to healthcare, social justice issues tend to be divisive. Even when an issue seems cut and dried, there are always two sides to every story, and governments and politicians rarely agree on which side is the right one. As you'll see in these articles, political figures and lawmakers often have complex views on the issues, whether they agree with them—as former First Lady Hillary Clinton discusses in her speech about women's rights—or disagree—as the Arizona lawmakers who wish to silence social justice education do.

"ARIZONA BILL WOULD BAN DISCUSSION OF SOCIAL JUSTICE, SOLIDARITY IN SCHOOLS," BY NIKA KNIGHT, FROM *COMMON DREAMS*, JANUARY 13, 2017

STATE LAWMAKER PROPOSES LEGISLATION THAT WOULD BAN CLASSES AND EXTRACURRICULAR ACTIVITES THAT "PROMOTE" SOCIAL JUSTICE OR SOLIDARITY

Arizona state representative Bob Thorpe, a Republican, has just proposed a bill that would ban any school courses or extracurricular activities that "promote" any kind of "social justice" or "solidarity" based on race, class, gender, politics, or religion.

The legislation, House Bill 2120, also appears to connect classes on social justice and solidarity with "promotion of the overthrow of the United States government," which it also explicitly outlaws.

Tucson.com reports that "Thorpe said Thursday his bill is aimed specifically at things like a 'privilege walk' exercise (pdf) sponsored by the University of Arizona and a course entitled 'Whiteness and Race Theory' at Arizona State University."

The law is sweeping yet fails to define many of its tenets—for example, it allows the teaching of "accurate" history of an ethnic group, but doesn't define who or what would determine what is accurate. And Arizonans fear that not only does it threaten students' and teachers' rights to freedom of expression and assembly, but that it would go so far as to outlaw all charity efforts and most student groups at schools around the state.

Brendan Mahoney, a member of the Phoenix Human Relations Commission, "wondered when social justice—the idea that people should work for the good of one another—became such a horrifying threat," writes local news outlet *AZCentral*:

> He says a high-school program to feed the homeless or a first-grade class project to send care packages to victims of natural disaster are examples of attempts to provide "social justice" toward "a class of people"—the very thing Thorpe's bill outlaws.
>
> "One could wonder how an elected official could sponsor something profoundly un-American," he said. "But reading between the lines, it's obvious the bill is targeting groups that our Legislature would rather not exist: Black Lives Matter, LGBT, undocumented, Dreamers."

In the Republican-dominated Arizona state legislature, the bill could very well pass, observers say, particularly as the state in 2010 already banned all ethnic studies classes.

As commentator Shaun King argues: "For all of their talk about local rights, it's deeply telling to see conservative lawmakers go so far as to say what individual dormitory directors and instructors can and cannot discuss with their students. Conservatives like Thorpe are fully willing to be control freaks when it protects white supremacy and cultural hegemony—then say they stand on the principles of local control when it benefits them."

Indeed, the Arizona bill comes as Republican-dominated legislatures across the nation are passing sweeping right-wing laws aimed at dismantling worker protections and civil rights, while a far-right president-elect prepares to be sworn in next week in Washington, D.C.

"I have a hunch this bill is not an anomaly, but a troubling sign of things to come," King says.

1. The Arizona state representative discussed in this article wants to ban lessons on social justice issues—like the lessons you're learning using this very book. If the representative's bill is passed, what impact do you think it will have on social justice and equality in Arizona?

2. As a student, why do you think it's important to be able to learn about social justice issues? How do you think your education would change if you weren't taught these topics in school?

"PAUL RYAN SAYS THE CATHOLIC CHARITY MODEL IS THE SOLUTION TO POVERTY. CATHOLICS DISAGREE," BY CLAIRE MARKHAM, FROM *COMMON DREAMS*, SEPTEMBER 2, 2016

Earlier this week, Speaker Paul Ryan and Senator Ron Johnson, both of Wisconsin, penned an op-ed stating—once again—their belief that charity and individual responsibility are the key to fighting poverty.

"This is how you fight poverty: person to person," they write.

To illustrate their point, they tell the story of The Joseph Project, a job assistance program run by the Greater Praise Church of God in Christ in Milwaukee. Ryan and Johnson praise The Joseph Project for providing vans that drive Milwaukeeans to Sheboygan County, where they can earn $15 an hour working a factory job. In Milwaukee, by contrast, these workers would likely earn just $8 or $9 an hour. The drive is an hour commute each way, but Ryan and Johnson assert: "That van represents the difference between poverty and opportunity."

While it's important that The Joseph Project is assisting these folks, it's disingenuous for the Speaker and the Senator to lift up this kind of program as the key to fighting poverty—and even a justification for overhauling our safety net.

The reality is that supporting an adequate minimum wage could also be the difference between poverty and opportunity for these workers. By supporting a minimum wage raise, Ryan could help put an end to poverty wages and save those same workers the two hours they spend each day riding in that van—giving them back some of the family time that Ryan cherishes so much in his own life.

To help the Speaker understand why his take on fighting poverty is so flawed, I suggest he return to the source he often cites as inspiration for his anti-poverty proposals: Catholicism.

In Sunday school classrooms across the country, young Catholics are taught the simplest versions of the

Catholic Church's complicated theology: God's love is represented by loving parents, Bible stories are boiled down to picture books, and stewardship of creation is taught by tending to one's own little plant. And one Sunday school classic, "The Two Feet of Love in Action," makes it clear that larger systemic solutions are integral to fighting poverty.

"There are two different, but complimentary, ways we can walk the path of love," the United States Conference of Catholic Bishops explains. "We call these 'The Two Feet of Love in Action.'" One foot is charity: direct service to help meet the immediate needs of individuals. The other foot is social justice: structural change to end the root causes of poverty.

The van is charity; the minimum wage hike is social justice.

Like Ryan, the Catholic Church values charity and applauds the commitment of faith communities like Greater Praise Church that provide direct assistance when people are in need. But, with its commitment to social justice as well, the Church might have some questions about why Ryan is trying to step with just one foot to end poverty. The bishops might even ask why the Speaker hasn't joined a living wage campaign—one of the examples of social justice on their Two Feet flier.

It serves Ryan's politics (and budgets) to let charity and other local efforts subsume broader anti-poverty initiatives, to diminish the work of the federal government in curbing poverty, and to pretend we can make meaningful change without making systemic change. But when people who are struggling turn to WIC, the EITC, or SNAP, that's not dependence—it's interdependence.

Giving from those who have more to those who have less on a person to person basis is charity, and it's good. Giving from those who have more to those who have less on a systemic level—making changes to ensure our tax code is fair, passing laws to increase the minimum wage, and ensuring our anti-poverty programs are more robust, not less—is justice, and it's necessary.

We need charity *and* social justice to end poverty. Any Sunday school student could teach Speaker Ryan that.

1. The author of the article discusses how Speaker Ryan believes that matters of social justice should be handled by individuals and private organizations, and not necessarily by government intervention. Can you think of examples where individuals were the best answer to a social justice issue? What about issues where the government was needed?

2. Speaker Ryan is specifically interested in how private organizations, such as religious charities, help people who are in poverty. What are some ways individuals can help people who are victims of economic inequality? What are ways in which the government can help these people?

"PHOENIX RESIDENTS, MAYOR AND POLICE VOW TO BUILD SOLUTIONS IN BLACK LIVES MATTER MEETING," BY COOPER GARDNER, FROM *CRONKITE NEWS*, JULY 20, 2016

PHOENIX – A teacher vowed to educate her students on race and social justice.

A young man promised to lead children to treat others fairly.

And Phoenix Mayor Greg Stanton pledged to hire a diverse police force.

The promises, written on note cards, came after about 500 people, including residents, Stanton, and police leaders attended a discussion earlier this week at Phillips Memorial CME Church.

The Rev. Reginald Walton, who hosted the event, said the point of "Moving Phoenix Forward" was to come up with solutions to an ongoing impasse over race.

"At some point in time, we have to come together and start working on solutions."

Stanton and Assistant Police Chief Mike Kurtenbach answered written questions ranging from a plea to train officers to interact better with the public and provide transparency if officers are accused of police misconduct.

Kurtenbach said the meeting was a first step in an ongoing conversation.

"As we walk out of here tonight, no one's going to pat themselves on the back and say we're done. This is how it starts."

A couple of people in the crowd that filled the church tried to shout comments but Walton asked people to follow a format of writing their questions on note cards and handing them to Phoenix officials.

Stanton defended the police department, saying it needs to improve but was recently praised by Attorney General Loretta Lynch for its approach to community policing.

Stanton mentioned that the department will hire 400 officers in the next few months, with diversifying the force in mind.

"We want the department to be as reflective as the incredible diversity that we are blessed to have in the community," Stanton said.

Walton, as the meeting ended, asked everyone to write down on note cards what they would do to provide bring justice and equality to the city.

The meeting ended with references to the teachings of Mahatma Gandhi.

"The change we seek, begins with me," Walton told the audience.

1. In an effort to help improve the problem of racial inequality in Phoenix, the mayor has promised to hire a more diverse police force. Based on what you've read in the above article, and what you know of the Black Lives Matter movement, what do you think are other ways communities like Phoenix can improve race relations and narrow the equality gap?

2. The article ends with a quote from Gandhi, "The change we seek, begins with me." What are some things you can do in your community to help promote social justice and equality?

"WOMEN'S RIGHTS ARE HUMAN RIGHTS," BY HILLARY RODHAM CLINTON, FROM THE UNITED NATIONS FOURTH WORLD CONFERENCE ON WOMEN, PLENARY SESSION IN BEIJING, CHINA, SEPTEMBER 5, 1995

Mrs. Mongella, Under Secretary Kittani, distinguished delegates and guests:

I would like to thank the Secretary General of the United Nations for inviting me to be part of the United Nations Fourth World Conference on Women. This is truly a celebration - a celebration of the contributions women make in every aspect of life: in the home, on the job, in their communities, as mothers, wives, sisters, daughters, learners, workers, citizens and leaders.

It is also a coming together, much the way women come together every day in every country.

We come together in fields and in factories. In village markets and supermarkets. In living rooms and board rooms.

Whether it is while playing with our children in the park, or washing clothes in a river, or taking a break at the office water cooler, we come together and talk about our aspirations and concerns. And time and again, our talk turns to our children and our families. However different we may be, there is far more that unites us than divides us. We share a common future. And we are here to find common ground so that we may help bring new dignity and respect to women and girls all over the world—and in so doing, bring new strength and stability to families as well.

By gathering in Beijing, we are focusing world attention on issues that matter most in the lives of women and their families: access to education, health care, jobs and credit, the chance to enjoy basic legal and human rights and participate fully in the political life of their countries.

There are some who question the reason for this conference.

Let them listen to the voices of women in their homes, neighborhoods, and workplaces.

There are some who wonder whether the lives of women and girls matter to economic and political progress around the globe.

Let them look at the women gathered here and at Huairou - the homemakers, nurses, teachers, lawyers, policymakers, and women who run their own businesses.

It is conferences like this that compel governments and people everywhere to listen, look and face the world's most pressing problems.

Wasn't it after the women's conference in Nairobi ten years ago that the world focused for the first time on the crisis of domestic violence?

Earlier today, I participated in a World Health Organization forum, where government officials, NGOs, and individual citizens are working on ways to address the health problems of women and girls.

Tomorrow, I will attend a gathering of the United Nations Development Fund for Women. There, the discussion will focus on local - and highly successful - programs that give hard-working women access to credit so they can improve their own lives and the lives of their families.

What we are learning around the world is that if women are healthy and educated, their families will flourish. If women are free from violence, their families will flourish. If women have a chance to work and earn as full and equal partners in society, their families will flourish.

And when families flourish, communities and nations will flourish.

That is why every woman, every man, every child, every family, and every nation on our planet has a stake in the discussion that takes place here.

Over the past 25 years, I have worked persistently on issues relating to women, children and families. Over the past two-and-a-half years, I have had the opportunity to learn more about the challenges facing women in my own country and around the world.

I have met new mothers in Jojakarta, Indonesia, who come together regularly in their village to discuss nutrition, family planning, and baby care.

I have met working parents in Denmark who talk about the comfort they feel in knowing that their children can be cared for in creative, safe, and nurturing after-school centers.

I have met women in South Africa who helped lead the struggle to end apartheid and are now helping build a new democracy.

I have met with the leading women of the Western Hemisphere who are working every day to promote literacy and better health care for the children of their countries.

I have met women in India and Bangladesh who are taking out small loans to buy milk cows, rickshaws, thread and other materials to create a livelihood for themselves and their families.

I have met doctors and nurses in Belarus and Ukraine who are trying to keep children alive in the aftermath of Chernobyl.

The great challenge of this Conference is to give voice to women everywhere whose experiences go unnoticed, whose words go unheard.

Women comprise more than half the world's population. Women are 70% percent of the world's poor, and two-thirds of those who are not taught to read and write.

Women are the primary caretakers for most of the world's children and elderly. Yet much of the work we do is not valued—not by economists, not by historians, not by popular culture, not by government leaders.

At this very moment, as we sit here, women around the world are giving birth, raising children, cooking meals, washing clothes, cleaning houses, planting crops, working on assembly lines, running companies, and running countries.

Women also are dying from diseases that should have been prevented or treated; they are watching their children succumb to malnutrition caused by poverty and economic deprivation; they are being denied the right to go to school by their own fathers and brothers; they are being forced into prostitution, and they are being barred from the bank lending office and banned from the ballot box.

Those of us who have the opportunity to be here have the responsibility to speak for those who could not.

As an American, I want to speak up for women in my own country—women who are raising children on the minimum wage, women who can't afford health care or child care, women whose lives are threatened by violence, including violence in their own homes.

I want to speak up for mothers who are fighting for good schools, safe neighborhoods, clean air and clean airwaves; for older women, some of them widows, who have raised their families and now find that their skills and life experiences are not valued in the workplace; for women who are working all night as nurses, hotel clerks, and fast food cooks so that they can be at home during the day with their kids; and for women everywhere who simply don't have time to do everything they are called upon to do each day.

Speaking to you today, I speak for them, just as each of us speaks for women around the world who are denied the chance to go to school, or see a doctor, or own property, or have a say about the direction of their lives, simply because they are women. The truth is that most women around the world work both inside and outside the home, usually by necessity.

We need to understand that there is no formula for how women should lead their lives. That is why we must respect the choices that each woman makes for herself and her family. Every woman deserves the chance to realize her God-given potential.

We also must recognize that women will never gain full dignity until their human rights are respected and protected.

Our goals for this Conference, to strengthen families and societies by empowering women to take greater control over their own destinies, cannot be fully achieved unless all governments - here and around the world - accept their responsibility to protect and promote internationally recognized human rights.

The international community has long acknowledged —and recently affirmed at Vienna—that both women and men are entitled to a range of protections and personal freedoms, from the right of personal security to the right to determine freely the number and spacing of the children they bear.

No one should be forced to remain silent for fear of religious or political persecution, arrest, abuse or torture.

Tragically, women are most often the ones whose human rights are violated.

Even in the late 20th century, the rape of women continues to be used as an instrument of armed conflict. Women and children make up a large majority of the world's refugees. When women are excluded from the political process, they become even more vulnerable to abuse.

I believe that, on the eve of a new millennium, it is time to break our silence. It is time for us to say here in Beijing, and the world to hear, that it is no longer acceptable to discuss women's rights as separate from human rights.

These abuses have continued because, for too long, the history of women has been a history of silence. Even today, there are those who are trying to silence our words.

The voices of this conference and of the women at Huairou must be heard loud and clear: It is a violation of human rights when babies are denied food, or drowned, or suffocated, or their spines broken, simply because they are born girls.

It is a violation of human rights when women and girls are sold into the slavery of prostitution.

It is a violation of human rights when women are doused with gasoline, set on fire and burned to death because their marriage dowries are deemed too small.

It is a violation of human rights when individual women are raped in their own communities and when thousands of women are subjected to rape as a tactic or prize of war.

It is a violation of human rights when a leading cause of death worldwide among women ages 14 to 44 is the violence they are subjected to in their own homes.

It is a violation of human rights when young girls are brutalized by the painful and degrading practice of genital mutilation.

It is a violation of human rights when women are denied the right to plan their own families, and that includes being forced to have abortions or being sterilized against their will.

If there is one message that echoes forth from this conference, it is that human rights are women's rights—and women's rights are human rights. Let us not forget that among those rights are the right to speak freely—and the right to be heard.

Women must enjoy the right to participate fully in the social and political lives of their countries if we want freedom and democracy to thrive and endure.

It is indefensible that many women in nongovernmental organizations who wished to participate in this conference have not been able to attend - or have been prohibited from fully taking part.

Let me be clear. Freedom means the right of people to assemble, organize, and debate openly. It means respecting the views of those who may disagree with the views of their governments. It means not taking citizens away from their loved ones and jailing them, mistreating them, or denying them their freedom or dignity because of the peaceful expression of their ideas and opinions.

In my country, we recently celebrated the 75th anniversary of women's suffrage. It took 150 years after the signing of our Declaration of Independence for women to win the right to vote.

It took 72 years of organized struggle on the part of many courageous women and men. It was one of America's most divisive philosophical wars. But it was also a bloodless war. Suffrage was achieved without a shot being fired.

We have also been reminded, in V-1 Day observances last weekend, of the good that comes when men and women join together to combat the forces of tyranny and build a better world.

We have seen peace prevail in most places for a half century. We have avoided another world war.

But we have not solved older, deeply rooted problems that continue to diminish the potential of half the world's population.

Now it is time to act on behalf of women everywhere. If we take bold steps to better the lives of women, we will be taking bold steps to better the lives of children and families too.

Families rely on mothers and wives for emotional support and care; families rely on women for labor in the home; and increasingly, families rely on women for income needed to raise healthy children and care for other relatives.

As long as discrimination and inequities remain so commonplace around the world - as long as girls and women are valued less, fed less, fed last, overworked, underpaid, not schooled and subjected to violence in and out of their homes - the potential of the human family to create a peaceful, prosperous world will not be realized.

Let this Conference be our - and the world's - call to action.

And let us heed the call so that we can create a world in which every woman is treated with respect and dignity, every boy and girl is loved and cared for equally, and every family has the hope of a strong and stable future.

Thank you very much.

God's blessings on you, your work and all who will benefit from it.

1. Former First Lady Clinton discusses in her speech the long fight for women's suffrage in the early twentieth century, and how many years it took for women to be considered equal to men in the voting booth in the United States. What are some social justice issues you think would be different if women hadn't been allowed to get involved in politics?

2. Clinton says "As long as discrimination and inequities remain so commonplace around the world—as long as girls and women are valued less, fed less, fed last, overworked, underpaid, not schooled and subjected to violence in and out of their homes—the potential of the human family to create a peaceful, prosperous world will not be realized." Her speech was written more than twenty years ago. Do you think that the issues she spoke about in 1995 are still problems today? What are some issues that face women that have a wider impact?

CHAPTER 3

WHAT THE COURTS SAY

Matters of social justice have been decided by the US court system since the 1800s, and many of those cases have reached the highest court in the land: the United States Supreme Court. While some decisions have been later overturned as the thinking has changed, other decisions have been groundbreaking for how quickly they've offered equality to a marginalized group. In this chapter, you'll look at cases that are both current and historic, upheld and later overturned, and discuss what impact these cases have had and what role they've played in how we view the importance of social justice.

EXCERPT FROM *BOY SCOUTS OF AMERICA ET AL. V. DALE*, 530 U.S. 640 (2000), FROM THE UNITED STATES SUPREME COURT, JUNE 28, 2000

The Boy Scouts is a private, not-for-profit organization engaged in instilling its system of values in young people. The Boy Scouts asserts that homosexual conduct is inconsistent with the values it seeks to instill. Respondent is James Dale, a former Eagle Scout whose adult membership in the Boy Scouts was revoked when the Boy Scouts learned that he is an avowed homosexual and gay rights activist. The New Jersey Supreme Court held that New Jersey's public accommodations law requires that the Boy Scouts readmit Dale. This case presents the question whether applying New Jersey's public accommodations law in this way violates the Boy Scouts' First Amendment right of expressive association. We hold that it does.

I

James Dale entered Scouting in 1978 at the age of eight by joining Monmouth Council's Cub Scout Pack 142. Dale became a Boy Scout in 1981 and remained a Scout until he turned 18. By all accounts, Dale was an exemplary Scout. In 1988, he achieved the rank of Eagle Scout, one of Scouting's highest honors.

Dale applied for adult membership in the Boy Scouts in 1989. The Boy Scouts approved his application for the position of assistant scoutmaster of Troop 73. Around the same time, Dale left home to attend Rutgers University. After arriving at Rutgers, Dale first acknowledged to himself and others that he is gay. He quickly became involved with, and eventually became the copresident of, the Rutgers University Lesbian/Gay Alliance. In 1990, Dale attended a seminar addressing the psychological and health needs of lesbian and gay teenagers. A newspaper covering the event interviewed Dale about his advocacy of homosexual teenagers' need for gay role models. In early July 1990, the newspaper published the interview and Dale's photograph over a caption identifying him as the copresident of the Lesbian/Gay Alliance.

Later that month, Dale received a letter from Monmouth Council Executive James Kay revoking his adult membership. Dale wrote to Kay requesting the reason for Monmouth Council's decision. Kay responded by letter that the Boy Scouts "specifically forbid membership to homosexuals." App. 137.

In 1992, Dale filed a complaint against the Boy Scouts in the New Jersey Superior Court. The complaint alleged that the Boy Scouts had violated New Jersey's public accommodations statute and its common law by revoking Dale's membership based solely on his sexual orientation. New Jersey's public accommodations statute prohibits, among other things, discrimination on the basis of sexual orientation in places of public accommodation. N. J. Stat. Ann. §§ 10:5-4 and 10:5-5 (West Supp. 2000); see Appendix, *infra*, at 661-663.

The New Jersey Superior Court's Chancery Division granted summary judgment in favor of the Boy Scouts. The court held that New Jersey's public accommodations law was inapplicable because the Boy Scouts was not a place of public accommodation, and that, alternatively, the Boy Scouts is a distinctly private group exempted from coverage under New Jersey's law. The court rejected Dale's common-law claim, holding that New Jersey's policy is embodied in the public accommodations law. The court also concluded that the Boy Scouts' position in respect of active homosexuality was clear and held that the First Amendment freedom of expressive association prevented the government from forcing the Boy Scouts to accept Dale as an adult leader.

The New Jersey Superior Court's Appellate Division affirmed the dismissal of Dale's common-law claim, but otherwise reversed and remanded for further proceedings. 308 N. J. Super. 516, 706 A. 2d 270 (1998). It held that New Jersey's public accommodations law applied to the Boy Scouts and that the Boy Scouts violated it. The Appellate Division rejected the Boy Scouts' federal constitutional claims.

The New Jersey Supreme Court affirmed the judgment of the Appellate Division. It held that the Boy Scouts was a place of public accommodation subject to the public accommodations law, that the organization was not exempt from the law under any of its express exceptions, and that the Boy Scouts violated the law by revoking Dale's membership based on his avowed homosexuality. After considering the state-law issues, the court addressed the Boy Scouts' claims that application of the public accommodations law in this case violated its federal constitutional rights "'to enter into and maintain ... intimate or private relationships ... [and] to associate for the purpose of engaging in protected speech.'" 160 N. J. 562, 605, 734 A. 2d 1196, 1219 (1999) (quoting *Board of Directors of Rotary Int'l* v. *Rotary Club of Duarte, 481* U. S. 537, 544 (1987)). With respect to the right to intimate association, the court concluded that the Boy Scouts' "large size, nonselectivity, inclusive rather than exclusive purpose, and practice of inviting or allowing nonmembers to attend meetings, establish that the organization is not 'sufficiently personal or private to warrant constitutional protection' under the freedom of intimate association." 160 N. J., at 608-609, 734 A. 2d, at 1221 (quoting *Duarte, supra*, at 546). With respect to the right of expressive association, the court "agree[d] that Boy Scouts expresses a belief in moral values and uses its activities to encourage the moral development of its members." 160 N. J., at 613, 734 A. 2d, at 1223. But the court concluded that it was "not persuaded ... that a shared goal of Boy Scout members is to associate in order to preserve the view that homosexuality is immoral." *Ibid.*, 734 A. 2d, at 1223-1224 (internal quotation marks omitted). Accordingly, the court held "that Dale's membership does not violate the Boy Scouts' right of expressive association because his inclusion would not 'affect in any significant way [the Boy Scouts'] existing members' ability to carry out their various purposes.'" *Id.*, at 615, 734 A. 2d, at 1225 (quoting *Duarte, supra*, at 548). The court also determined that New Jersey has a compelling interest in eliminating "the destructive consequences of discrimination from our society," and that its public accommodations law abridges no more speech than is necessary to accomplish its purpose. 160 N. J., at 619-620,734 A. 2d, at 1227-1228. Finally, the court addressed the Boy Scouts' reliance on *Hurley* v. *IrishAmerican Gay, Lesbian and Bisexual Group of Boston, Inc.*, 515 U. S. 557 (1995), in support of its claimed

First Amendment right to exclude Dale. The court determined that *Hurley* did not require deciding the case in favor of the Boy Scouts because "the reinstatement of Dale does not compel Boy Scouts to express any message." 160 N. J., at 624, 734 A. 2d, at 1229.

We granted the Boy Scouts' petition for certiorari to determine whether the application of New Jersey's public accommodations law violated the First Amendment. 528 U. S. 1109 (2000).

II

In *Roberts v. United States Jaycees*, 468 U. S. 609, 622 (1984), we observed that "implicit in the right to engage in activities protected by the First Amendment" is "a corresponding right to associate with others in pursuit of a wide variety of political, social, economic, educational, religious, and cultural ends." This right is crucial in preventing the majority from imposing its views on groups that would rather express other, perhaps unpopular, ideas. See *ibid.* (stating that "protection of the right to expressive association is "especially important in preserving political and cultural diversity and in shielding dissident expression from suppression by the majority"). Government actions that may unconstitutionally burden this freedom may take many forms, one of which is "intrusion into the internal structure or affairs of an association" like a "regulation that forces the group to accept members it does not desire." *Id.*, at 623. Forcing a group to accept certain members may impair the ability of the group to express those views, and only those views, that it intends to express. Thus, "[f]reedom of association ... plainly presupposes a freedom not to associate." *Ibid.*

The forced inclusion of an unwanted person in a group infringes the group's freedom of expressive association if the presence of that person affects in a significant way the group's ability to advocate public or private viewpoints. *New York State Club Assn., Inc. v. City of New York*, 487 U. S. 1, 13 (1988). But the freedom of expressive association, like many freedoms, is not absolute. We have held that the freedom could be overridden "by regulations adopted to serve compelling state interests, unrelated to the suppression of ideas, that cannot be achieved through means significantly less restrictive of associational freedoms." *Roberts, supra*, at 623.

To determine whether a group is protected by the First Amendment's expressive associational right, we must determine whether the group engages in "expressive association." The First Amendment's protection of expressive association is not reserved for advocacy groups. But to come within its ambit, a group must engage in some form of expression, whether it be public or private.

Because this is a First Amendment case where the ultimate conclusions of law are virtually inseparable from findings of fact, we are obligated to independently review the factual record to ensure that the state court's judgment does not unlawfully intrude on free expression. See *Hurley, supra*, at 567-568. The record reveals the following. The Boy Scouts is a private, nonprofit organization. According to its mission statement:

> "It is the mission of the Boy Scouts of America to serve others by helping to instill values in young people and, in other ways, to prepare them to make ethical choices over their lifetime in achieving their full potential.

> "The values we strive to instill are based on those found in the Scout Oath and Law:
>
> "Scout Oath
>
> "On my honor I will do my best
>
> "To do my duty to God and my country "and to obey the Scout Law;
>
> "To help other people at all times;
>
> "To keep myself physically strong, "mentally awake, and morally straight.
>
> "Scout Law
>
> "A Scout is:
>
> "Trustworthy Obedient
>
> "Loyal Cheerful
>
> "Helpful Thrifty
>
> "Friendly Brave
>
> "Courteous Clean
>
> "Kind Reverent." App. 184.

Thus, the general mission of the Boy Scouts is clear: "[T]o instill values in young people." *Ibid.* The Boy Scouts seeks to instill these values by having its adult leaders spend time with the youth members, instructing and engaging them in activities like camping, archery, and fishing. During the time spent with the youth members, the scoutmasters and assistant scoutmasters inculcate them with the Boy

Scouts' values—both expressly and by example. It seems indisputable that an association that seeks to transmit such a system of values engages in expressive activity. See *Roberts, supra*, at 636 (O'Connor, J., concurring) ("Even the training of outdoor survival skills or participation in community service might become expressive when the activity is intended to develop good morals, reverence, patriotism, and a desire for self-improvement").

Given that the Boy Scouts engages in expressive activity, we must determine whether the forced inclusion of Dale as an assistant scoutmaster would significantly affect the Boy Scouts' ability to advocate public or private viewpoints. This inquiry necessarily requires us first to explore, to a limited extent, the nature of the Boy Scouts' view of homosexuality.

The values the Boy Scouts seeks to instill are "based on" those listed in the Scout Oath and Law. App. 184. The Boy Scouts explains that the Scout Oath and Law provide "a positive moral code for living; they are a list of `do's' rather than `don'ts.' " Brief for Petitioners 3. The Boy Scouts asserts that homosexual conduct is inconsistent with the values embodied in the Scout Oath and Law, particularly with the values represented by the terms "morally straight" and "clean."

Obviously, the Scout Oath and Law do not expressly mention sexuality or sexual orientation. See *supra*, at 649. And the terms "morally straight" and "clean" are by no means self-defining. Different people would attribute to those terms very different meanings. For example, some people may believe that engaging in homosexual conduct is not at odds with being "morally straight" and "clean." And others may believe that engaging in homosexual conduct is contrary to being "morally straight" and "clean." The Boy Scouts says it falls within the latter category.

The New Jersey Supreme Court analyzed the Boy Scouts' beliefs and found that the "exclusion of members solely on the basis of their sexual orientation is inconsistent with Boy Scouts' commitment to a diverse and `representative' membership . . . [and] contradicts Boy Scouts' overarching objective to reach `all eligible youth.' " 160 N. J., at 618, 734 A. 2d, at 1226. The court concluded that the exclusion of members like Dale "appears antithetical to the organization's goals and philosophy." *Ibid.* But our cases reject this sort of inquiry; it is not the role of the courts to reject a group's expressed values because they disagree with those values or find them internally inconsistent. See *Democratic Party of United States v. Wisconsin ex rel. La Follette,* 450 U. S. 107, 124 (1981) ("[A]s is true of all expressions of First Amendment freedoms, the courts may not interfere on the ground that they view a particular expression as unwise or irrational"); see also *Thomas v. Review Bd. of Indiana Employment Security Div.,* 450 U. S. 707, 714 (1981) ("[R]eligious beliefs need not be acceptable, logical, consistent, or comprehensible to others in order to merit First Amendment protection").

The Boy Scouts asserts that it "teach[es] that homosexual conduct is not morally straight," Brief for Petitioners 39, and that it does "not want to promote homosexual conduct as a legitimate form of behavior," Reply Brief for Petitioners 5. We accept the Boy Scouts' assertion. We need not inquire further to determine the nature of the Boy Scouts' expression with respect to homosexuality. But because the record before us contains written evidence of the Boy Scouts' viewpoint, we look to it as instructive, if only on the question of the sincerity of the professed beliefs.

A 1978 position statement to the Boy Scouts' Executive Committee, signed by Downing B. Jenks, the President of the Boy Scouts, and Harvey L. Price, the Chief Scout Executive, expresses the Boy Scouts' "official position" with regard to "homosexuality and Scouting":

> "Q. May an individual who openly declares himself to be a homosexual be a volunteer Scout leader?
>
> "A. No. The Boy Scouts of America is a private, membership organization and leadership therein is a privilege and not a right. We do not believe that homosexuality and leadership in Scouting are appropriate. We will continue to select only those who in our judgment meet our standards and qualifications for leadership." App. 453-454.

Thus, at least as of 1978—the year James Dale entered Scouting—the official position of the Boy Scouts was that avowed homosexuals were not to be Scout leaders.

A position statement promulgated by the Boy Scouts in 1991 (after Dale's membership was revoked but before this litigation was filed) also supports its current view:

> "We believe that homosexual conduct is inconsistent with the requirement in the Scout Oath that a Scout be morally straight and in the Scout Law that a Scout be clean in word and deed, and that homosexuals do not provide a desirable role model for Scouts." *Id.*, at 457.

This position statement was redrafted numerous times but its core message remained consistent. For example, a 1993 position statement, the most recent in the record, reads, in part:

> "The Boy Scouts of America has always reflected the expectations that Scouting families have had for the organization. We do not believe that homosexuals provide a role model consistent with these expectations. Accordingly, we do not allow for the registration of avowed homosexuals as members or as leaders of the BSA." *Id.*, at 461.

The Boy Scouts publicly expressed its views with respect to homosexual conduct by its assertions in prior litigation. For example, throughout a California case with similar facts filed in the early 1980's, the Boy Scouts consistently asserted the same position with respect to homosexuality that it asserts today. See *Curran v. Mount Diablo Council of Boy Scouts of America*, No. C-365529 (Cal. Super. Ct., July 25, 1991); 48 Cal. App. 4th 670, 29 Cal. Rptr. 2d 580 (1994); 17 Cal. 4th 670, 952 P. 2d 218 (1998). We cannot doubt that the Boy Scouts sincerely holds this view.

We must then determine whether Dale's presence as an assistant scoutmaster would significantly burden the Boy Scouts' desire to not "promote homosexual conduct as a legitimate form of behavior." Reply Brief for Petitioners 5. As we give deference to an association's assertions regarding the nature of its expression, we must also give deference to an association's view of what would impair its expression. See, *e. g., La Follette, supra*, at 123-124 (considering whether a Wisconsin law burdened the National Party's associational rights and stating that "a State, or a court, may not constitutionally substitute its own judgment for that of the Party"). That is not to say that an expressive association can erect a shield against antidiscrimination laws simply by asserting that mere acceptance of a member from a particular group would impair its message. But here Dale, by his own admission, is one of a group of gay Scouts who have "become leaders in their community and are open and honest about their sexual orientation." App. 11. Dale was the copresident of a gay and lesbian organization at college and remains a gay rights activist. Dale's presence in the Boy Scouts would, at the very least, force the organization to send a message, both to the youth members and the world, that the Boy Scouts accepts homosexual conduct as a legitimate form of behavior.

Hurley is illustrative on this point. There we considered whether the application of Massachusetts' public accommodations law to require the organizers of a private St. Patrick's Day parade to include among the marchers an IrishAmerican gay, lesbian, and bisexual group, GLIB, violated the parade organizers' First Amendment rights. We noted that the parade organizers did not wish to exclude the GLIB members because of their sexual orientations, but because they wanted to march behind a GLIB banner. We observed:

> "[A] contingent marching behind the organization's banner would at least bear witness to the fact that some Irish are gay, lesbian, or bisexual, and the presence of the organized marchers would suggest their view that people of their sexual orientations have as much claim to unqualified social acceptance as heterosexuals . . . . The parade's organizers may not believe these facts

> about Irish sexuality to be so, or they may object to unqualified social acceptance of gays and lesbians or have some other reason for wishing to keep GLIB's message out of the parade. But whatever the reason, it boils down to the choice of a speaker not to propound a particular point of view, and that choice is presumed to lie beyond the government's power to control." 515 U. S., at 574-575.

Here, we have found that the Boy Scouts believes that homosexual conduct is inconsistent with the values it seeks to instill in its youth members; it will not "promote homosexual conduct as a legitimate form of behavior." Reply Brief for Petitioners 5. As the presence of GLIB in Boston's St. Patrick's Day parade would have interfered with the parade organizers' choice not to propound a particular point of view, the presence of Dale as an assistant scoutmaster would just as surely interfere with the Boy Scout's choice not to propound a point of view contrary to its beliefs.

The New Jersey Supreme Court determined that the Boy Scouts' ability to disseminate its message was not significantly affected by the forced inclusion of Dale as an assistant scoutmaster because of the following findings:

> "Boy Scout members do not associate for the purpose of disseminating the belief that homosexuality is immoral; Boy Scouts discourages its leaders from disseminating *any* views on sexual issues; and Boy Scouts includes sponsors and members who subscribe to different views in respect of homosexuality." 160 N. J., at 612, 734 A. 2d, at 1223.

We disagree with the New Jersey Supreme Court's conclusion drawn from these findings.

First, associations do not have to associate for the "purpose" of disseminating a certain message in order to be entitled to the protections of the First Amendment. An association must merely engage in expressive activity that could be impaired in order to be entitled to protection. For example, the purpose of the St. Patrick's Day parade in *Hurley* was not to espouse any views about sexual orientation, but we held that the parade organizers had a right to exclude certain participants nonetheless.

Second, even if the Boy Scouts discourages Scout leaders from disseminating views on sexual issues—a fact that the Boy Scouts disputes with contrary evidence—the First Amendment protects the Boy Scouts' method of expression. If the Boy Scouts wishes Scout leaders to avoid questions of sexuality and teach only by example, this fact does not negate the sincerity of its belief discussed above.

Third, the First Amendment simply does not require that every member of a group agree on every issue in order for the group's policy to be "expressive association." The Boy Scouts takes an official position with respect to homosexual conduct, and that is sufficient for First Amendment purposes. In this same vein, Dale makes much of the claim that the Boy Scouts does not revoke the membership of heterosexual Scout leaders that openly disagree with the Boy Scouts' policy on sexual orientation. But if this is true, it is irrelevant. [1] The presence of an avowed homosexual and gay rights activist in an assistant scoutmaster's uniform sends a distinctly different message from the presence of a heterosexual assistant scoutmaster who is on record as disagreeing with Boy Scouts policy. The Boy Scouts has a First Amendment right to choose to send one message but not the other. The fact that the organization does not trumpet its views from the housetops, or that it tolerates dissent within its ranks, does not mean that its views receive no First Amendment protection.

Having determined that the Boy Scouts is an expressive association and that the forced inclusion of Dale would significantly affect its expression, we inquire whether the application of New Jersey's public accommodations law to require that the Boy Scouts accept Dale as an assistant scoutmaster runs afoul of the Scouts' freedom of expressive association. We conclude that it does.

State public accommodations laws were originally enacted to prevent discrimination in traditional places of public accommodation—like inns and trains. See, *e. g., Hurley, supra*, at 571-572 (explaining the history of Massachusetts' public accommodations law); *Romer v. Evans*, 517 U. S. 620, 627-629 (1996) (describing the evolution of public accommodations laws). Over time, the public accommodations laws have expanded to cover more places. [2] New Jersey's statutory definition of "`[a] place of public accommodation' " is extremely broad. The term is said to "include, but not be limited to," a list of over 50 types of places. N. J. Stat. Ann. § 10:5-5(l) (West Supp. 2000); see Appendix, *infra*, at 661— 663. Many on the list are what one would expect to be places where the public is invited. For example, the statute includes as places of public accommodation taverns, restaurants, retail shops, and public libraries. But the statute also includes places that often may not carry with them open invitations to the public, like summer camps and roof gardens. In this case, the New Jersey Supreme Court went a step further and applied its public accommodations law to a private entity without even attempting to tie the term "place" to a physical location. [3] As the definition of "public accommodation" has expanded from clearly commercial entities, such as restaurants, bars, and hotels, to membership organizations such as the Boy Scouts, the potential for conflict between state public accommodations laws and the First Amendment rights of organizations has increased.

We recognized in cases such as *Roberts* and *Duarte* that States have a compelling interest in eliminating discrimination against women in public accommodations. But in each of these cases we went on to conclude that the enforcement of these statutes would not materially interfere with the ideas that the organization sought to express. In *Roberts*, we said "[i]ndeed, the Jaycees has failed to demonstrate . . . any serious burdens on the male members' freedom of expressive association." 468 U. S., at 626. In *Duarte*, we said:

> "[I]mpediments to the exercise of one's right to choose one's associates can violate the right of association protected by the First Amendment. In this case, however, the evidence fails to demonstrate that admitting women to Rotary Clubs will affect in any significant way the existing members' ability to carry out their various purposes." 481 U. S., at 548 (internal quotation marks and citations omitted).

We thereupon concluded in each of these cases that the organizations' First Amendment rights were not violated by the application of the States' public accommodations laws.

In *Hurley*, we said that public accommodations laws "are well within the State's usual power to enact when a legislature has reason to believe that a given group is the target of discrimination, and they do not, as a general matter, violate the First or Fourteenth Amendments." 515 U. S., at 572. But we went on to note that in that case "the Massachusetts [public accommodations] law has been applied in a peculiar way" because "any contingent of protected individuals with a message would have the right to participate in petitioners' speech, so that the communication produced by the private organizers would be shaped by all those protected by the law who wished to join in with some expressive demonstration of their own." *Id.*, at 572-573. And in the associational freedom cases such as *Roberts*, *Duarte*, and *New York State Club Assn.*, after finding a compelling state interest, the Court went on to examine whether or not the application of the state law would impose any "serious burden" on the organization's rights of expressive association. So in these cases, the associational interest in freedom of expression has been set on one side of the scale, and the State's interest on the other.

Dale contends that we should apply the intermediate standard of review enunciated in *United States v. O'Brien*, 391 U. S. 367 (1968), to evaluate the competing interests. There the Court enunciated a four-part test for review of a governmental regulation that has only an incidental effect on protected speech—in that case the symbolic burning of a draft card. A law prohibiting the destruction of draft cards only incidentally affects the free speech rights of those who happen to use a violation of that law as a symbol of protest. But New Jersey's public accommodations law directly and immediately affects associational rights, in this case associational rights that enjoy First Amendment protection. Thus, *O'Brien* is inapplicable.

In *Hurley*, we applied traditional First Amendment analysis to hold that the application of the Massachusetts public accommodations law to a parade violated the First Amendment rights of the parade organizers. Although we did not explicitly deem the parade in *Hurley* an expressive association, the analysis we applied there is similar to the analysis we apply here. We have already concluded that a state requirement that the Boy Scouts retain Dale as an assistant scoutmaster would significantly burden the organization's right to oppose or disfavor homosexual conduct. The state interests embodied in New Jersey's public accommodations law do not justify such a severe intrusion on the Boy Scouts' rights to freedom of expressive association. That being the case, we hold that the First Amendment prohibits the State from imposing such a requirement through the application of its public accommodations law. [4]

Justice Stevens' dissent makes much of its observation that the public perception of homosexuality in this country has changed. See post, at 699-700. Indeed, it appears that homosexuality has gained greater societal acceptance. See *ibid.* But this is scarcely an argument for denying First Amendment protection to those who refuse to accept these views. The First Amendment protects expression, be it of the popular variety or not. See, *e. g., Texas v. Johnson*, 491 U. S. 397 (1989) (holding that Johnson's conviction for burning the American flag violates the First Amendment); *Brandenburg v. Ohio*, 395 U. S. 444 (1969) (*per curiam*) (holding that a Ku Klux Klan leader's conviction for advocating unlawfulness as a means of political reform violates the First Amendment).

And the fact that an idea may be embraced and advocated by increasing numbers of people is all the more reason to protect the First Amendment rights of those who wish to voice a different view.

Justice Stevens' extolling of Justice Brandeis' comments in *New State Ice Co. v. Liebmann*, 285 U. S. 262, 311 (1932) (dissenting opinion); see post, at 664, 700, confuses two entirely different principles. In New State Ice, the Court struck down an Oklahoma regulation prohibiting the manufacture, sale, and distribution of ice without a license. Justice Brandeis, a champion of state experimentation in the economic realm, dissented. But Justice Brandeis was never a champion of state experimentation in the suppression of free speech. To the contrary, his First Amendment commentary provides compelling support for the Court's opinion in this case. In speaking of the Founders of this Nation, Justice Brandeis emphasized that they "believed that freedom to think as you will and to speak as you think are means indispensable to the discovery and spread of political truth." *Whitney v. California*, 274 U. S. 357, 375 (1927) (concurring opinion). He continued:

> "Believing in the power of reason as applied through public discussion, they eschewed silence coerced by law—the argument of force in its worst form. Recognizing the occasional tyrannies of governing majorities, they amended the Constitution so that free speech and assembly should be guaranteed." *Id.*, at 375-376.

We are not, as we must not be, guided by our views of whether the Boy Scouts' teachings with respect to homosexual conduct are right or wrong; public or judicial disapproval of a tenet of an organization's expression does not justify the State's effort to compel the organization to accept members where such acceptance would derogate from the organization's expressive message. "While the law is free to promote all sorts of conduct in place of harmful behavior, it is not free to interfere with speech for no better reason than promoting an approved message or discouraging a disfavored one, however enlightened either purpose may strike the government." *Hurley*, 515 U. S., at 579.

The judgment of the New Jersey Supreme Court is reversed, and the case is remanded for further proceedings not inconsistent with this opinion.

It is so ordered.

1. While previous cases held that discrimination against people based on sexual orientation are unacceptable, the justices decided that the Boy Scouts could bar gay men from joining because they are a private group. After reading the court's decision, do you believe that allowing the Boy Scouts to bar members upholds the organization's rights, or does it infringe on the potential member's rights?

2. The justices relied heavily on the *Hurley* case, which said groups did not have to permit participants whose message they disagreed with, and that forcing them to do so would be forcing them to appear as if they agree. Do you think, based on the facts cited by the Court, that the Boy Scouts should be permitted to ban gay members because of this case? Or do you think the *Hurley* case cited applies only to demonstrations and not to an organization? Explain your reasoning.

EXCERPT FROM *UNITED STATES V. VIRGINIA ET AL.*, 518 U.S. 515 (1996), FROM THE UNITED STATES SUPREME COURT, JUNE 26, 1996

SUMMARY

Virginia Military Institute (VMI) is the sole single-sex school among Virginia's public institutions of higher learning. VMI's distinctive mission is to produce "citizen-soldiers," men prepared for leadership in civilian life and in military service. Using an "adversative method" of training not available elsewhere in Virginia, VMI endeavors to instill physical and mental discipline in its cadets and impart to them a strong moral code. Reflecting the high value alumni place on their VMI training,

VMI has the largest per-student endowment of all public undergraduate institutions in the Nation. The United States sued Virginia and VMI, alleging that VMI's exclusively male admission policy violated the Fourteenth Amendment's Equal Protection Clause. The District Court ruled in VMI's favor. The Fourth Circuit reversed and ordered Virginia to remedy the constitutional violation. In response, Virginia proposed a parallel program for women: Virginia Women's Institute for Leadership (VWIL), located at Mary Baldwin College, a private liberal arts school for women. The District Court found that Virginia's proposal satisfied the Constitution's equal protection requirement, and the Fourth Circuit affirmed. The appeals court deferentially reviewed Virginia's plan and determined that provision of single-gender educational options was a legitimate objective. Maintenance of single-sex programs, the court concluded, was essential to that objective. The court recognized, however, that its analysis risked bypassing equal protection scrutiny, so it fashioned an additional test, asking whether VMI and VWIL students would receive "substantively comparable" benefits. Although the Court of Appeals acknowledged that the VWIL degree lacked the historical benefit and prestige of a VMI degree, the court nevertheless found the educational opportunities at the two schools sufficiently comparable.

[...]

III

The cross-petitions in this suit present two ultimate issues. First, does Virginia's exclusion of women from the educational opportunities provided by VMI—extraordinary opportunities for military training and civilian leadership development—deny to women "capable of all of the individual activities required of VMI cadets," 766 F. Supp., at 1412, the equal protection of the laws guaranteed by the Fourteenth Amendment? Second, if VMI's "unique" situation, *id.*, at 1413—as Virginia's sole single-sex public institution of higher education—offends the Constitution's equal protection principle, what is the remedial requirement?

IV

We note, once again, the core instruction of this Court's pathmarking decisions in *J. E. B. v. Alabama ex rel. T. B.*, 511 U. S. 127, 136-137, and n. 6 (1994), and *Mississippi Univ. for Women*, 458 U. S., at 724 (internal quotation marks omitted): Parties who seek to defend gender-based government action must demonstrate an "exceedingly persuasive justification" for that action.

Today's skeptical scrutiny of official action denying rights or opportunities based on sex responds to volumes of history. As a plurality of this Court acknowledged a generation ago, "our Nation has had a long and unfortunate history of sex discrimination." *Frontiero v. Richardson*, 411 U. S. 677, 684 (1973). Through a century plus three decades and more of that history, women did not count among voters composing "We the People"; [5] not until 1920 did women gain a constitutional right to the franchise. *Id.*, at 685. And for a half century thereafter, it remained the prevailing doctrine that government, both federal and state, could withhold from women opportunities accorded men so long as any "basis in reason" could be conceived for the discrimination. See, *e. g., Goesaert v. Cleary*, 335 U. S. 464, 467 (1948) (rejecting challenge of female tavern owner and her daughter to Michigan law denying bartender licenses to females—except for wives and daughters of male tavern owners; Court would not "give ear" to the contention that "an unchivalrous desire of male bartenders to . . . monopolize the calling" prompted the legislation).

In 1971, for the first time in our Nation's history, this Court ruled in favor of a woman who complained that her State had denied her the equal protection of its laws. *Reed v. Reed*, 404 U. S. 71, 73 (holding unconstitutional Idaho Code prescription that, among "`several persons claiming and equally entitled to administer [a decedent's estate], males must be preferred to females' "). Since *Reed*, the Court has repeatedly recognized that neither federal nor state government acts compatibly with the equal protection principle when a law or official policy denies to women, simply because they are women, full citizenship stature—equal opportunity to aspire, achieve, participate in and contribute to society based on their individual talents and capacities. See, *e. g., Kirchberg v. Feenstra*, 450 U. S. 455, 462-463 (1981) (affirming invalidity of Louisiana law that made husband "head and master" of property jointly owned with his wife, giving him unilateral right to dispose of such property without his wife's consent); *Stanton v. Stanton*, 421 U. S. 7 (1975) (invalidating Utah requirement that parents support boys until age 21, girls only until age 18).

Without equating gender classifications, for all purposes, to classifications based on race or national origin, [6] the Court, in post-*Reed* decisions, has carefully inspected official action that closes a door or denies opportunity to women (or to men). See *J. E. B.*, 511 U. S., at 152 (Kennedy, J., concurring in judgment) (case law evolving since 1971 "reveal[s] a strong presumption that gender classifications are invalid"). To summarize the Court's current directions for cases of official classification based on gender: Focusing on the differential treatment or denial of opportunity for which relief is sought, the reviewing court must determine whether the proffered justification is "exceedingly persuasive." The burden of justification is demanding and it rests entirely on the State. See *Mississippi Univ. for Women*, 458 U. S., at 724. The State must show "at least that the [challenged] classification serves `important governmental objectives and that the discriminatory means employed' are `substantially related to the achievement of those objectives.' " *Ibid.* (quoting *Wengler v. Druggists Mut. Ins. Co.* , 446 U. S. 142, 150 (1980)). The justification must be genuine, not hypothesized or invented post hoc in response to litigation. And it must not rely on overbroad generalizations about the different talents, capacities, or preferences of males and females. See *Weinberger v. Wiesenfeld*, 420 U. S. 636, 643, 648 (1975); *Califano v. Goldfarb*, 430 U. S. 199, 223-224 (1977) (Stevens, J., concurring in judgment).

The heightened review standard our precedent establishes does not make sex a proscribed classification. Supposed "inherent differences" are no longer accepted as a ground for race or national origin classifications. See *Loving v. Virginia*, 388 U. S. 1 (1967). Physical differences between men and women, however, are enduring: "[T]he two sexes are not fungible; a community made up exclusively of one [sex] is different from a community composed of both." *Ballard v. United States*, 329 U. S. 187, 193 (1946).

"Inherent differences" between men and women, we have come to appreciate, remain cause for celebration, but not for denigration of the members of either sex or for artificial constraints on an individual's opportunity. Sex classifications may be used to compensate women "for particular economic disabilities [they have] suffered," *Califano v. Webster*, 430 U. S. 313, 320 (1977) (*per curiam*), to "promot[e] equal employment opportunity," see *California Fed. Sav. & Loan Assn. v. Guerra*, 479 U. S. 272, 289 (1987), to advance full development of the talent and capacities of our Nation's people. [7] But such classifications may not be used, as they once were, see *Goesaert*, 335 U. S., at 467, to create or perpetuate the legal, social, and economic inferiority of women.

Measuring the record in this case against the review standard just described, we conclude that Virginia has shown no "exceedingly persuasive justification" for excluding all women from the citizen-soldier training afforded by VMI. We therefore affirm the Fourth Circuit's initial judgment, which held that Virginia had violated the Fourteenth Amendment's Equal Protection Clause. Because the remedy proffered by Virginia—the Mary Baldwin VWIL program—does not cure the constitutional violation, i.e., it does not provide equal opportunity, we reverse the Fourth Circuit's final judgment in this case.

V

The Fourth Circuit initially held that Virginia had advanced no state policy by which it could justify, under equal protection principles, its determination "to afford VMI's unique type of program to men and not to women." 976

F. 2d, at 892. Virginia challenges that "liability" ruling and asserts two justifications in defense of VMI's exclusion of women. First, the Commonwealth contends, "single-sex education provides important educational benefits," Brief for Cross-Petitioners 20, and the option of single-sex education contributes to "diversity in educational approaches," *id.*, at 25. Second, the Commonwealth argues, "the unique VMI method of character development and leadership training," the school's adversative approach, would have to be modified were VMI to admit women. Id., at 33-36 (internal quotation marks omitted). We consider these two justifications in turn.

A

Single-sex education affords pedagogical benefits to at least some students, Virginia emphasizes, and that reality is uncontested in this litigation. [8] Similarly, it is not disputed that diversity among public educational institutions can serve the public good. But Virginia has not shown that VMI was established, or has been maintained, with a view to diversifying, by its categorical exclusion of women, educational opportunities within the Commonwealth. In cases of this genre, our precedent instructs that "benign" justifications proffered in defense of categorical exclusions will not be accepted automatically; a tenable justification must describe actual state purposes, not rationalizations for actions in fact differently grounded. See *Wiesenfeld*, 420 U. S., at 648, and n. 16 ("mere recitation of a benign [or] compensatory purpose" does not block "inquiry into the actual purposes" of government-maintained gender-based classifications); Goldfarb, 430 U. S., at 212-213 (rejecting government-proffered purposes after "inquiry into the actual purposes" (internal quotation marks omitted)).

Mississippi Univ. for Women is immediately in point. There the State asserted, in justification of its exclusion of men from a nursing school, that it was engaging in "educational affirmative action" by "compensat[ing] for discrimination against women." 458 U. S., at 727. Undertaking a "searching analysis," *id.*, at 728, the Court found no close resemblance between "the alleged objective" and "the actual purpose underlying the discriminatory classification," *id.*, at 730. Pursuing a similar inquiry here, we reach the same conclusion.

Neither recent nor distant history bears out Virginia's alleged pursuit of diversity through single-sex educational options. In 1839, when the Commonwealth established VMI, a range of educational opportunities for men and women was scarcely contemplated. Higher education at the time was considered dangerous for women; [9] reflecting widely held views about women's proper place, the Nation's first universities and colleges—for example, Harvard in Massachusetts, William and Mary in Virginia—admitted only men. See E. Farello, A History of the Education of Women in the United States 163 (1970). VMI was not at all novel in this respect: In admitting no women, VMI followed the lead of the Commonwealth's flagship school, the University of Virginia, founded in 1819.

"[N]o struggle for the admission of women to a state university," a historian has recounted, "was longer drawn out, or developed more bitterness, than that at the University of Virginia." 2 T. Woody, A History of Women's Education in the United States 254 (1929) (History of

Women's Education). In 1879, the State Senate resolved to look into the possibility of higher education for women, recognizing that Virginia "`has never, at any period of her history,' " provided for the higher education of her daughters, though she "`has liberally provided for the higher education of her sons.' " *Ibid.* (quoting 10 Educ. J. Va. 212 (1879)). Despite this recognition, no new opportunities were instantly open to women. [10]

Virginia eventually provided for several women's seminaries and colleges. Farmville Female Seminary became a public institution in 1884. See *supra*, at 521, n. 2. Two women's schools, Mary Washington College and James Madison University, were founded in 1908; another, Radford University, was founded in 1910. 766 F. Supp., at 1418-1419. By the mid-1970's, all four schools had become coeducational. *Ibid.*

Debate concerning women's admission as undergraduates at the main university continued well past the century's midpoint. Familiar arguments were rehearsed. If women were admitted, it was feared, they "would encroach on the rights of men; there would be new problems of government, perhaps scandals; the old honor system would have to be changed; standards would be lowered to those of other coeducational schools; and the glorious reputation of the university, as a school for men, would be trailed in the dust." 2 History of Women's Education 255.

Ultimately, in 1970, "the most prestigious institution of higher education in Virginia," the University of Virginia, introduced coeducation and, in 1972, began to admit women on an equal basis with men. See *Kirstein v. Rector and Visitors of Univ. of Virginia*, 309 F. Supp. 184, 186 (ED Va. 1970). A three-judge Federal District Court confirmed:

> "Virginia may not now deny to women, on the basis of sex, educational opportunities at the Charlottesville campus that are not afforded in other institutions operated by the [S]tate." *Id.*, at 187.

Virginia describes the current absence of public single-sex higher education for women as "an historical anomaly." Brief for Cross-Petitioners 30. But the historical record indicates action more deliberate than anomalous: First, protection of women against higher education; next, schools for women far from equal in resources and stature to schools for men; finally, conversion of the separate schools to coeducation. The state legislature, prior to the advent of this controversy, had repealed "[a]ll Virginia statutes requiring individual institutions to admit only men or women." 766 F. Supp., at 1419. And in 1990, an official commission, "legislatively established to chart the future goals of higher education in Virginia," reaffirmed the policy "`of affording broad access" while maintaining "autonomy and diversity.' " 976 F. 2d, at 898-899 (quoting Report of the Virginia Commission on the University of the 21st Century). Significantly, the commission reported:

> "`Because colleges and universities provide opportunities for students to develop values and learn from role models, it is extremely important that they deal with faculty, staff, and students without regard to sex, race, or ethnic origin.' " *Id.*, at 899 (emphasis supplied by Court of Appeals deleted).

This statement, the Court of Appeals observed, "is the only explicit one that we have found in the record in which the Commonwealth has expressed itself with respect to gender distinctions." *Ibid.*

Our 1982 decision in *Mississippi Univ. for Women* prompted VMI to reexamine its male-only admission policy. See 766 F. Supp., at 1427-1428. Virginia relies on that reexamination as a legitimate basis for maintaining VMI's single-sex character. See Reply Brief for Cross-Petitioners 6. A Mission Study Committee, appointed by the VMI Board of Visitors, studied the problem from October 1983 until May 1986, and in that month counseled against "change of VMI status as a single-sex college." See 766 F. Supp., at 1429 (internal quotation marks omitted). Whatever internal purpose the Mission Study Committee served—and however well meaning the framers of the report—we can hardly extract from that effort any commonwealth policy evenhandedly to advance diverse educational options. As the District Court observed, the Committee's analysis "primarily focuse[d] on anticipated difficulties in attracting females to VMI," and the report, overall, supplied "very little indication of how th[e] conclusion was reached." *Ibid.*

In sum, we find no persuasive evidence in this record that VMI's male-only admission policy "is in furtherance of a state policy of `diversity.' " See 976 F. 2d, at 899. No such policy, the Fourth Circuit observed, can be discerned from the movement of all other public colleges and universities in Virginia away from single-sex education. See ibid. That court also questioned "how one institution with autonomy, but with no authority over any other state institution, can give effect to a state policy of diversity among institutions." Ibid. A purpose genuinely to advance an array of educational options, as the Court of Appeals recognized, is not served by VMI's historic and constant plan—a plan to "affor[d] a unique educational benefit only to males." *Ibid*. However "liberally" this plan serves the Commonwealth's sons, it makes no provision whatever for her daughters. That is not *equal* protection.

B

Virginia next argues that VMI's adversative method of training provides educational benefits that cannot be made available, unmodified, to women. Alterations to accommodate women would necessarily be "radical," so "drastic," Virginia asserts, as to transform, indeed "destroy," VMI's program. See Brief for Cross-Petitioners 34-36. Neither sex would be favored by the transformation, Virginia maintains: Men would be deprived of the unique opportunity currently available to them; women would not gain that opportunity because their participation would "eliminat[e] the very aspects of [the] program that distinguish [VMI] from . . . other institutions of higher education in Virginia." *Id.*, at 34.

The District Court forecast from expert witness testimony, and the Court of Appeals accepted, that coeducation would materially affect "at least these three aspects of VMI's program—physical training, the absence of privacy, and the adversative approach." 976 F. 2d, at 896-897. And it is uncontested that women's admission would require accommodations, primarily in arranging housing assignments and physical training programs for female cadets. See Brief for Cross-Respondent 11, 29-30. It is also undisputed, however, that "the VMI methodology could be used to educate women." 852 F. Supp., at 481. The District Court even allowed that some women may prefer it to the methodology a women's college might pursue. See *ibid.* "[S]ome women, at least, would want to attend [VMI] if they had the opportunity," the District Court recognized, 766 F.

Supp., at 1414, and "some women," the expert testimony established, "are capable of all of the individual activities required of VMI cadets," id., at 1412. The parties, furthermore, agree that "some women can meet the physical standards [VMI] now impose[s] on men." 976 F. 2d, at 896. In sum, as the Court of Appeals stated, "neither the goal of producing citizen soldiers," VMI's *raison d'être,* "nor VMI's implementing methodology is inherently unsuitable to women." *Id.,* at 899.

In support of its initial judgment for Virginia, a judgment rejecting all equal protection objections presented by the United States, the District Court made "findings" on "gender-based developmental differences." 766 F. Supp., at 1434-1435. These "findings" restate the opinions of Virginia's expert witnesses, opinions about typically male or typically female "tendencies." *Id.,* at 1434. For example, "[m]ales tend to need an atmosphere of adversativeness," while "[f]emales tend to thrive in a cooperative atmosphere." *Ibid.* "I'm not saying that some women don't do well under [the] adversative model," VMI's expert on educational institutions testified, "undoubtedly there are some [women] who do"; but educational experiences must be designed "around the rule," this expert maintained, and not "around the exception." *Ibid.* (internal quotation marks omitted).

The United States does not challenge any expert witness estimation on average capacities or preferences of men and women. Instead, the United States emphasizes that time and again since this Court's turning point decision in *Reed v. Reed,* 404 U. S. 71 (1971), we have cautioned reviewing courts to take a "hard look" at generalizations or "tendencies" of the kind pressed by Virginia, and relied upon by the District Court. See O'Connor, Portia's Progress, 66 N. Y. U. L. Rev. 1546, 1551 (1991). State actors controlling gates to opportunity, we have instructed, may not exclude qualified individuals based on "fixed notions concerning the roles and abilities of males and females." *Mississippi Univ. for Women*, 458 U. S., at 725; see *J. E. B.*, 511 U. S., at 139, n. 11 (equal protection principles, as applied to gender classifications, mean state actors may not rely on "overbroad" generalizations to make "judgments about people that are likely to . . . perpetuate historical patterns of discrimination").

It may be assumed, for purposes of this decision, that most women would not choose VMI's adversative method. As Fourth Circuit Judge Motz observed, however, in her dissent from the Court of Appeals' denial of rehearing en banc, it is also probable that "many men would not want to be educated in such an environment." 52 F. 3d, at 93. (On that point, even our dissenting colleague might agree.) Education, to be sure, is not a "one size fits all" business. The issue, however, is not whether "women—or men—should be forced to attend VMI"; rather, the question is whether the Commonwealth can constitutionally deny to women who have the will and capacity, the training and attendant opportunities that VMI uniquely affords. *Ibid.*

The notion that admission of women would downgrade VMI's stature, destroy the adversative system and, with it, even the school, [11] is a judgment hardly proved, [12] a prediction hardly different from other "self-fulfilling prophec[ies]," see *Mississippi Univ. for Women*, 458 U. S., at 730, once routinely used to deny rights or opportunities. When women first sought admission to the bar and access to legal education, concerns of the same order were expressed. For example, in 1876, the Court of

Common Pleas of Hennepin County, Minnesota, explained why women were thought ineligible for the practice of law. Women train and educate the young, the court said, which

> "forbids that they shall bestow that time (early and late) and labor, so essential in attaining to the eminence to which the true lawyer should ever aspire. It cannot therefore be said that the opposition of courts to the admission of females to practice . . . is to any extent the outgrowth of . . . `old fogyism[.]' . . . [I]t arises rather from a comprehension of the magnitude of the responsibilities connected with the successful practice of law, and a desire to *grade up* the profession." In re Application of Martha Angle Dorsett to Be Admitted to Practice as Attorney and Counselor at Law (Minn. C. P. Hennepin Cty., 1876), in The Syllabi, Oct. 21, 1876, pp. 5, 6 (emphasis added).

A like fear, according to a 1925 report, accounted for Columbia Law School's resistance to women's admission, although

> "[t]he faculty . . . never maintained that women could not master legal learning . . . . No, its argument has been . . . more practical. If women were admitted to the Columbia Law School, [the faculty] said, then the choicer, more manly and red-blooded graduates of our great universities would go to the Harvard Law School!" The Nation, Feb. 18, 1925, p. 173.

Medical faculties similarly resisted men and women as partners in the study of medicine. See R. Morantz-Sanchez, Sympathy and Science: Women Physicians in American Medicine 51-54, 250 (1985); see also M. Walsh, "Doctors Wanted: No Women Need Apply" 121-122 (1977) (quoting E. Clarke, Medical

Education of Women, 4 Boston Med. & Surg. J. 345, 346 (1869) ("`God forbid that I should ever see men and women aiding each other to display with the scalpel the secrets of the reproductive system . . . .' ")); cf. *supra*, at 536-537, n. 9. More recently, women seeking careers in policing encountered resistance based on fears that their presence would "undermine male solidarity," see F. Heidensohn, Women in Control? 201 (1992); deprive male partners of adequate assistance, see *id.*, at 184-185; and lead to sexual misconduct, see C. Milton et al., Women in Policing 32-33 (1974). Field studies did not confirm these fears. See Heidensohn, *supra*, at 92-93; P. Bloch & D. Anderson, Policewomen on Patrol: Final Report (1974).

Women's successful entry into the federal military academies, [13] and their participation in the Nation's military forces, [14] indicate that Virginia's fears for the future of VMI 545*545 may not be solidly grounded. [15] The Commonwealth's justification for excluding all women from "citizen-soldier" training for which some are qualified, in any event, cannot rank as "exceedingly persuasive," as we have explained and applied that standard.

Virginia and VMI trained their argument on "means" rather than "end," and thus misperceived our precedent. Single-sex education at VMI serves an "important governmental objective," they maintained, and exclusion of women is not only "substantially related," it is essential to that objective. By this notably circular argument, the "straightforward" test *Mississippi Univ. for Women* described, see 458 U. S., at 724-725, was bent and bowed.

The Commonwealth's misunderstanding and, in turn, the District Court's, is apparent from VMI's mission: to produce "citizen-soldiers," individuals

> "`imbued with love of learning, confident in the functions and attitudes of leadership, possessing a high sense of public service, advocates of the American democracy and free enterprise system, and ready . . . to defend their country in time of national peril.' " 766 F. Supp., at 1425 (quoting Mission Study Committee of the VMI Board of Visitors, Report, May 16, 1986).

Surely that goal is great enough to accommodate women, who today count as citizens in our American democracy equal in stature to men. Just as surely, the Commonwealth's great goal is not substantially advanced by women's categorical exclusion, in total disregard of their individual merit, from the Commonwealth's premier "citizen-soldier" corps. [16] Virginia, in sum, "has fallen far short of establishing the `exceedingly persuasive justification,' " *Mississippi Univ. for Women*, 458 U. S., at 731, that must be the solid base for any gender-defined classification.

1. The Court decided that the Virginia Military Institute could not prohibit women from entering the school, nor could it provide a "separate but equal" facility for women wishing to attend the service institute, because the separate school would not offer the women equal opportunities or education. However, other schools today are still able to offer single-sex education. What do you think makes the case of VMI different?

2. Based on what VMI and the state of Virginia argued, do you think they had a case for keeping VMI a men-only institution? What impact do you think a different ruling would have had on women's fight for equality in later years?

EXCERPT FROM *PLESSY V. FERGUSON*, 163 U.S. 537 (1896), FROM THE UNITED STATES SUPREME COURT, MAY 18, 1896

Mr. Justice Harlan, dissenting.

By the Louisiana statute, the validity of which is here involved, all railway companies (other than street railroad companies) carrying passengers in that State are required to have separate but equal accommodations for white and colored persons, "by providing two or more passenger coaches for each passenger train, or by dividing the passenger coaches by a partition so as to secure separate accommodations."

Under this statute, no colored person is permitted to occupy a seat in a coach assigned to white persons; nor any white person, to occupy a seat in a coach assigned to colored persons. The managers of the railroad are not allowed to exercise any discretion in the premises, but are required to assign each passenger to some coach or compartment set apart for the exclusive use of his race. If a passenger insists upon going into a coach or compartment not set apart for persons of his race, he is subject to be fined, or to be imprisoned in the parish jail. Penalties are prescribed for the refusal or neglect of the officers, directors, conductors and employees of railroad companies to comply with the provisions of the act.

Only "nurses attending children of the other race" are excepted from the operation of the statute. No exception is made of colored attendants travelling with adults. A white man is not permitted to have his colored servant with him in the same coach, even if his condition of health requires the constant, personal assistance of such servant. If a colored maid insists upon riding in the same coach with a white woman whom she has been employed to serve, and who may need her personal attention while travelling, she is subject to be fined or imprisoned for such an exhibition of zeal in the discharge of duty.

While there may be in Louisiana persons of different races who are not citizens of the United States, the words in the act, "white and colored races," necessarily include all citizens of the United States of both races residing in that State. So that we have before us a state enactment that compels, under penalties, the separation of the two races in railroad passenger coaches, and makes it a crime for a citizen of either race to enter a coach that has been assigned to citizens of the other race.

Thus, the State regulates the use of a public highway by citizens of the United States solely upon the basis of race.

However apparent the injustice of such legislation may be, we have only to consider whether it is consistent with the Constitution of the United States.

That a railroad is a public highway, and that the corporation which owns or operates it is in the exercise of public functions, is not, at this day, to be disputed. Mr.

Justice Nelson, speaking for this court in *New Jersey Steam Navigation Co. v. Merchants' Bank*, 6 How. 344, 382, said that a common carrier was in the exercise "of a sort of public office, and has public duties to perform, from which he should not be permitted to exonerate himself without the assent of the parties concerned." Mr. Justice Strong, delivering the judgment of this court in *Olcott v. The Supervisors*, 16 Wall. 678, 694, said: "That railroads, though constructed by private corporations and owned by them, are public highways, has been the doctrine of nearly all the courts ever since such conveniences for passage and transportation have had any existence. Very early the question arose whether a State's right of eminent domain could be exercised by a private corporation created for the purpose of constructing a railroad. Clearly it could not, unless taking land for such a purpose by such an agency is taking land for public use. The right of eminent domain nowhere justifies taking property for a private use. Yet it is a doctrine universally accepted that a state legislature may authorize a private corporation to take land for the construction of such a road, making compensation to the owner. What else does this doctrine mean if not that building a railroad, though it be built by a private corporation, is an act done for a public use?"

So, in *Township of Pine Grove v. Talcott*, 19 Wall. 666, 676: "Though the corporation [a railroad company] was private, its work was public, as much so as if it were to be constructed by the State." So, in *Inhabitants of Worcester v. Western Railroad Corporation*, 4 Met. 564: "The establishment of that great thoroughfare is regarded as a public work, established by public authority, intended for the public use and benefit, the use of which is secured to the whole community, and constitutes, therefore, like a canal, turnpike or highway, a public easement." It is true that the real and personal property, necessary to the establishment and management of the railroad, is vested in the corporation; but it is in trust for the public."

In respect of civil rights, common to all citizens, the Constitution of the United States does not, I think, permit any public authority to know the race of those entitled to be protected in the enjoyment of such rights. Every true man has pride of race, and under appropriate circumstances when the rights of others, his equals before the law, are not to be affected, it is his privilege to express such pride and to take such action based upon it as to him seems proper. But I deny that any legislative body or judicial tribunal may have regard to the race of citizens when the civil rights of those citizens are involved. Indeed, such legislation, as that here in question, is inconsistent not only with that equality of rights which pertains to citizenship, National and State, but with the personal liberty enjoyed by every one within the United States.

The Thirteenth Amendment does not permit the withholding or the deprivation of any right necessarily inhering in freedom. It not only struck down the institution of slavery as previously existing in the United States, but it prevents the imposition of any burdens or disabilities that constitute badges of slavery or servitude. It decreed universal civil freedom in this country. This court has so adjudged. But that amendment having been found inadequate to the protection of the rights of those who had been in slavery, it was followed by the Fourteenth Amendment, which added greatly to the dignity and glory of American citizenship, and to the security of personal liberty, by declaring that "all persons born or naturalized in the United States, and subject to the jurisdiction thereof, are citizens of the United States and of the State wherein they reside," and that "no State shall make or enforce any law which shall abridge the privileges or immunities of citizens of the United States; nor shall any State deprive any person of life, liberty or property without due process of law, nor deny to any person within its jurisdiction the equal protection of the laws."

These two amendments, if enforced according to their true intent and meaning, will protect all the civil rights that pertain to freedom and citizenship. Finally, and to the end that no citizen should be denied, on account of his race, the privilege of participating in the political control of his country, it was declared by the Fifteenth Amendment that "the right of citizens of the United States to vote shall not be denied or abridged by the United States or by any State on account of race, color or previous condition of servitude."

These notable additions to the fundamental law were welcomed by the friends of liberty throughout the world. They removed the race line from our governmental systems. They had, as this court has said, a common purpose, namely, to secure "to a race recently emancipated, a race that through many generations have been held in slavery, all the civil rights that the superior race enjoy."

They declared, in legal effect, this court has further said, "that the law in the States shall be the same for the black as for the white; that all persons, whether colored or white, shall stand equal before the laws of the States, and, in regard to the colored race, for whose protection the amendment was primarily designed, that no discrimination shall be made against them by law because of their color."

We also said: "The words of the amendment, it is true, are prohibitory, but they contain a necessary implication of a positive immunity, or right, most valuable to the colored race — the right to exemption from unfriendly legislation against them distinctively as colored — exemption from legal discriminations, implying inferiority in civil society, lessening the security of their enjoyment of the rights which others enjoy, and discriminations which are steps towards reducing them to the condition of a subject race." It was, consequently, adjudged that a state law that excluded citizens of the colored race from juries, because of their race and however well qualified in other respects to discharge the duties of jurymen, was repugnant to the Fourteenth Amendment. *Strauder v. West Virginia*, 100 U.S. 303, 306, 307; *Virginia v. Rives*, 100 U.S. 313; *Ex parte Virginia*, 100 U.S. 339; *Neal v. Delaware*, 103 U.S. 370, 386; *Bush v. Kentucky*, 107 U.S. 110, 116. At the present term, referring to the previous adjudications, this court declared that "underlying all of those decisions is the principle that the Constitution of the United States, in its present form, forbids, so far as civil and political rights are concerned, discrimination by the General Government or the States against any citizen because of his race. All citizens are equal before the law." *Gibson v. Mississippi*, 162 U.S. 565.

The decisions referred to show the scope of the recent amendments of the Constitution. They also show that it is not within the power of a State to prohibit colored citizens, because of their race, from participating as jurors in the administration of justice.

It was said in argument that the statute of Louisiana does not discriminate against either race, but prescribes a rule applicable alike to white and colored citizens. But this argument does not meet the difficulty. Every one knows that the statute in question had its origin in the purpose, not so much to exclude white persons from railroad cars occupied by blacks, as to exclude colored people from coaches occupied by or assigned to white persons. Railroad corporations of Louisiana did not make discrimination among whites in the matter of accommodation for travellers. The thing to accomplish was, under the guise of giving equal accommodation for whites and blacks, to compel the latter to keep to themselves while travelling in railroad passenger coaches. No one would be so wanting in candor as to assert the contrary. The fundamental objection, therefore, to the statute is that it interferes with the personal freedom of citizens. "Personal liberty," it has been well said, "consists in the power of locomotion, of changing situation, or removing one's person to whatsoever places one's own inclination may direct, without imprisonment or restraint, unless by due course of law." 1 Bl. Com. *134. If a white man and a black man choose to occupy the same public conveyance on a public highway, it is their right to do so, and no government, proceeding alone on grounds of race, can prevent it without infringing the personal liberty of each.

It is one thing for railroad carriers to furnish, or to be required by law to furnish, equal accommodations for all whom they are under a legal duty to carry. It is quite another thing for government to forbid citizens of the white and black races from travelling in the same public conveyance, and to punish officers of railroad companies for permitting persons of the two races to occupy the same passenger coach. If a State can prescribe, as a rule of civil conduct, that whites and blacks shall not travel as passengers in the same railroad coach, why may it not so regulate the use of the streets of its cities and towns as to compel white citizens to keep on one side of a street and black citizens to keep on the other? Why may it not, upon like grounds, punish whites and blacks who ride together in street cars or in open vehicles on a public road or street? Why may it not require sheriffs to assign whites to one side of a court-room and blacks to the other? And why may it not also prohibit the commingling of the two races in the galleries of legislative halls or in public assemblages convened for the consideration of the political questions of the day? Further, if this statute of Louisiana is consistent with the personal liberty of citizens, why may not the State require the separation in railroad coaches of native and naturalized citizens of the United States, or of Protestants and Roman Catholics?

The answer given at the argument to these questions was that regulations of the kind they suggest would be unreasonable, and could not, therefore, stand before the law. Is it meant that the determination of questions of legislative power depends upon the inquiry whether the statute whose validity is questioned is, in the judgment of the courts, a reasonable one, taking all the circumstances into consideration? A statute may be unreasonable merely because a sound public policy forbade its enactment. But I do not understand that the courts have anything to do with the policy or expediency of legislation. A statute may be valid, and yet, upon grounds of public policy, may well be characterized as unreasonable. Mr. Sedgwick correctly states the rule when he says that the legislative intention being clearly ascertained, "the courts have no other duty to perform than to execute the legislative will, without any regard to their views as to the wisdom or justice of the particular enactment." Stat. & Const. Constr. 324. There is a dangerous tendency in these latter days to enlarge the functions of the courts, by means of judicial interference with the will of the people as expressed by the legislature. Our institutions have the distinguishing characteristic that the three departments of government are coordinate and separate. Each must keep within the limits defined by the Constitution. And the courts best discharge their duty by executing the will of the law-making power, constitutionally expressed, leaving the results of legislation to be dealt with by the people through their representatives. Statutes must always have a reasonable construction. Sometimes they are to be construed strictly; sometimes, liberally, in order to carry out the legislative 559*559 will. But however construed, the intent of the legislature is to be respected, if the particular statute in question is valid, although the courts, looking at the public interests, may conceive the statute to be both unreasonable and impolitic. If the power exists to enact a statute, that ends the matter so far as the courts are concerned. The adjudged cases in which statutes have been held to be void, because unreasonable, are those in which the means employed by the legislature were not at all germane to the end to which the legislature was competent.

The white race deems itself to be the dominant race in this country. And so it is, in prestige, in achievements, in education, in wealth and in power. So, I doubt not, it will continue to be for all time, if it remains true to its great heritage and holds fast to the principles of constitutional liberty. But in view of the Constitution, in the eye of the law, there is in this country no superior, dominant, ruling class of citizens. There is no caste here. Our Constitution is color-blind, and neither knows nor tolerates classes among citizens. In respect of civil rights, all citizens are equal before the law. The humblest is the peer of the most powerful. The law regards man as man, and takes no account of his surroundings or of his color when his civil rights as guaranteed by the supreme law of the land are involved. It is, therefore, to be regretted that this high tribunal, the final expositor of the fundamental law of the land, has reached the conclusion that it is competent for a State to regulate the enjoyment by citizens of their civil rights solely upon the basis of race.

In my opinion, the judgment this day rendered will, in time, prove to be quite as pernicious as the decision made by this tribunal in the *Dred Scott* case. It was adjudged in that case that the descendants of Africans who were imported into this country and sold as slaves were not included nor intended to be included under the word "citizens" in the Constitution, and could not claim any of the rights and privileges which that instrument provided for and secured to citizens of the United States; that at the time of the adoption of the Constitution they were "considered as a subordinate and inferior class of beings, who had been subjugated by the dominant race, and, whether emancipated or not, yet remained subject to their authority, and had no rights or privileges but such as those who held the power and the government might choose to grant them." 19 How. 393, 404. The recent amendments of the Constitution, it was supposed, had eradicated these principles from our institutions. But it seems that we have yet, in some of the States, a dominant race — a superior class of citizens, which assumes to regulate the enjoyment of civil rights, common to all citizens, upon the basis of race. The present decision, it may well be apprehended, will not only stimulate aggressions, more or less brutal and irritating, upon the admitted rights of colored citizens, but will encourage the belief that it is possible, by means of state enactments, to defeat the beneficent purposes which the people of the United States had in view when they adopted the recent amendments of the Constitution, by one of which the blacks of this country were made citizens of the United States and of the States in which they respectively reside, and whose privileges and immunities, as citizens, the States are forbidden to abridge. Sixty millions of whites are in no danger from the presence here of eight millions of blacks. The destinies of the two races, in this country, are indissolubly linked together, and the interests of both require that the common government of all shall not permit the seeds of race hate to be planted under the sanction of law. What can more certainly arouse race hate, what more certainly create and perpetuate a feeling of distrust between these races, than state enactments, which, in fact, proceed on the ground that colored citizens are so inferior and degraded that they cannot be allowed to sit in public coaches occupied by white citizens? That, as all will admit, is the real meaning of such legislation as was enacted in Louisiana.

The sure guarantee of the peace and security of each race is the clear, distinct, unconditional recognition by our governments, National and State, of every right that inheres in civil freedom, and of the equality before the law of all citizens of the United States without regard to race. State enactments, regulating the enjoyment of civil rights, upon the basis of race, and cunningly devised to defeat legitimate results of the war, under the pretence of recognizing equality of rights, can have no other result than to render permanent peace impossible, and to keep alive a conflict of races, the continuance of which must do harm to all concerned. This question is not met by the suggestion that social equality cannot exist between the white and black races in this country. That argument, if it can be properly regarded as one, is scarcely worthy of consideration; for social equality no more exists between two races when travelling in a passenger coach or a public highway than when members of the same races sit by each other in a street car or in the jury box, or stand or sit with each other in a political assembly, or when they use in common the streets of a city or town, or when they are in the same room for the purpose of having their names placed on the registry of voters, or when they approach the ballot-box in order to exercise the high privilege of voting.

There is a race so different from our own that we do not permit those belonging to it to become citizens of the United States. Persons belonging to it are, with few exceptions, absolutely excluded from our country. I allude to the Chinese race. But by the statute in question, a Chinaman can ride in the same passenger coach with white citizens of the United States, while citizens of the black race in Louisiana, many of whom, perhaps, risked their lives for the preservation of the Union, who are entitled, by law, to participate in the political control of the State and nation, who are not excluded, by law or by reason of their race, from public stations of any kind, and who have all the legal rights that belong to white citizens, are yet declared to be criminals, liable to imprisonment, if they ride in a public coach occupied by citizens of the white race. It is scarcely just to say that a colored citizen should not object to occupying a public coach assigned to his own race. He does not object, nor, perhaps, would he object to separate coaches for his race, if his rights under the law were recognized. But he objects, and ought never to cease objecting to the proposition, that citizens of the white and black races can be adjudged criminals because they sit, or claim the right to sit, in the same public coach on a public highway.

The arbitrary separation of citizens, on the basis of race, while they are on a public highway, is a badge of servitude wholly inconsistent with the civil freedom and the equality before the law established by the Constitution. It cannot be justified upon any legal grounds.

If evils will result from the commingling of the two races upon public highways established for the benefit of all, they will be infinitely less than those that will surely come from state legislation regulating the enjoyment of civil rights upon the basis of race. We boast of the freedom enjoyed by our people above all other peoples. But it is difficult to reconcile that boast with a state of the law which, practically, puts the brand of servitude and degradation upon a large class of our fellow-citizens, our equals before the law. The thin disguise of "equal" accommodations for passengers in railroad coaches will not mislead any one, nor atone for the wrong this day done.

The result of the whole matter is, that while this court has frequently adjudged, and at the present term has recognized the doctrine, that a State cannot, consistently with the Constitution of the United States, prevent white and black citizens, having the required qualifications for jury service, from sitting in the same jury box, it is now solemnly held that a State may prohibit white and black citizens from sitting in the same passenger coach on a public highway, or may require that they be separated by a "partition," when in the same passenger coach. May it not now be reasonably expected that astute men of the dominant race, who affect to be disturbed at the possibility that the integrity of the white race may be corrupted, or that its supremacy will be imperilled, by contact on public highways with black people, will endeavor to procure statutes requiring white and black jurors to be separated in the jury box by a "partition," and that, upon retiring from the court room to consult as to their verdict, such partition, if it be a moveable one, shall be taken to their consultation room, and set up in such way as to prevent black jurors from coming too close to their brother jurors of the white race. If the "partition" used in the court room happens to be stationary, provision could be made for screens with openings through 563*563 which jurors of the two races could confer as to their verdict without coming into personal contact with each other. I cannot see but that, according to the principles this day announced, such state legislation, although conceived in hostility to, and enacted for the purpose of humiliating citizens of the United States of a particular race, would be held to be consistent with the Constitution.

I do not deem it necessary to review the decisions of state courts to which reference was made in argument. Some, and the most important, of them are wholly inapplicable, because rendered prior to the adoption of the last amendments of the Constitution, when colored people had very few rights which the dominant race felt obliged to respect. Others were made at a time when public opinion, in many localities, was dominated by the institution of slavery; when it would not have been safe to do justice to the black man; and when, so far as the rights of blacks were concerned, race prejudice was, practically, the supreme law of the land. Those decisions cannot be guides in the era introduced by the recent amendments of the supreme law, which established universal civil freedom, gave citizenship to all born or naturalized in the United States and residing here, obliterated the race line from our systems of governments, National and State, and placed our free institutions upon the broad and sure foundation of the equality of all men before the law.

I am of opinion that the statute of Louisiana is inconsistent with the personal liberty of citizens, white and black, in that State, and hostile to both the spirit and letter of the Constitution of the United States. If laws of like character should be enacted in the several States of the Union, the effect would be in the highest degree mischievous. Slavery, as an institution tolerated by law would, it is true, have disappeared from our country, but there would remain a power in the States, by sinister legislation, to interfere with the full enjoyment of the blessings of freedom; to regulate civil rights, common to all citizens, upon the basis of race; and to place in a condition of legal inferiority a large body of American citizens, now constituting a part of the political community called the People of the United States, for whom, and by whom through representatives, our government is administered. Such a system is inconsistent with the guarantee given by the Constitution to each State of a republican form of government, and may be stricken down by Congressional action, or by the courts in the discharge of their solemn duty to maintain the supreme law of the land, anything in the constitution or laws of any State to the contrary notwithstanding.

For the reasons stated, I am constrained to withhold my assent from the opinion and judgment of the majority.

1. In his dissenting opinion, Justice Harlan says it matters most not whether "separate but equal" is moral or right or even socially acceptable, but whether it is constitutional, and he believes it is not. Based on the facts cited by Justice Harlan, do you think the Court made the right decision, constitutionally, for the time?

2. Nearly sixty years after the *Plessy v. Ferguson* case was decided, *Brown v. Board of Education* (1954) overturned the case, deciding that "separate but equal," when it came to the races, was not equal. Without reading the new case, what do you think could have led to the Supreme Court changing its mind, even though the Constitution hadn't changed?

EXCERPT FROM *PEÑA-RODRIGUEZ V. COLORADO*, 580 U.S. ___ (2017), FROM THE SUPREME COURT OF THE UNITED STATES, MARCH 6, 2017

A Colorado jury convicted petitioner Peña-Rodriguez of harassment and unlawful sexual contact. Following the discharge of the jury, two jurors told defense counsel that, during deliberations, Juror H. C. had expressed anti-Hispanic bias toward petitioner and petitioner's alibi witness. Counsel, with the trial court's supervision, obtained affidavits from the two jurors describing a number of biased statements by H. C. The court acknowledged H. C.'s apparent bias but denied petitioner's motion for a new trial on the grounds that Colorado Rule of Evidence 606(b) generally prohibits a juror from testifying as to statements made during deliberations in a proceeding inquiring into the validity of the verdict. The Colorado Court of Appeals affirmed, agreeing that H. C.'s alleged statements did not fall within an exception to Rule 606(b). The Colorado Supreme Court also affirmed, relying on *Tanner* v. *United States*, 483 U. S. 107, and *Warger* v. *Shauers*, 574 U. S. ___, both of which rejected constitutional challenges to the federal no-impeachment rule as applied to evidence of juror misconduct or bias.

III

It must become the heritage of our Nation to rise above racial classifications that are so inconsistent with our commitment to the equal dignity of all persons. This imperative to purge racial prejudice from the administration of justice was given new force and direction by the ratification of the Civil War Amendments.

"[T]he central purpose of the Fourteenth Amendment was to eliminate racial discrimination emanating from official sources in the States." *McLaughlin v. Florida*, 379 U. S. 184, 192 (1964). In the years before and after the ratification of the Fourteenth Amendment, it became clear that racial discrimination in the jury system posed a particular threat both to the promise of the Amendment and to the integrity of the jury trial. "Almost immediately after the Civil War, the South began a practice that would continue for many decades: All-white juries punished black defendants particularly harshly, while simultaneously refusing to punish violence by whites, including Ku Klux Klan members, against blacks and Republicans." Forman, Juries and Race in the Nineteenth Century, 113 Yale L. J. 895, 909–910 (2004). To take one example, just in the years 1865 and 1866, all-white juries in Texas decided a total of 500 prosecutions of white defendants charged with killing African-Americans. All 500 were acquitted. *Id.*, at 916. The stark and unapologetic nature of race-motivated outcomes challenged the American belief that "the jury was a bulwark of liberty," *id.*, at 909, and prompted Congress to pass legislation to integrate the jury system and to bar persons from eligibility for jury service if they had conspired to deny the civil rights of African- Americans, id., at 920–930. Members of Congress stressed that the legislation was necessary to preserve the right to a fair trial and to guarantee the equal protection of the laws. *Ibid.*

The duty to confront racial animus in the justice system is not the legislature's alone. Time and again, this

Court has been called upon to enforce the Constitution's guarantee against state-sponsored racial discrimination in the jury system. Beginning in 1880, the Court interpreted the Fourteenth Amendment to prohibit the exclusion of jurors on the basis of race. *Strauder v. West Virginia*, 100 U. S. 303, 305–309 (1880). The Court has repeatedly struck down laws and practices that systematically exclude racial minorities from juries. See, *e.g., Neal v. Delaware*, 103 U.S. 370 (1881); *Hollins v. Oklahoma*, 295 U.S. 394 (1935) (*per curiam*); *Avery v. Georgia*, 345 U. S. 559 (1953); *Hernandez v. Texas*, 347 U. S. 475 (1954); *Castaneda v. Partida*, 430 U. S. 482 (1977). To guard against discrimination in jury selection, the Court has ruled that no litigant may exclude a prospective juror on the basis of race. *Batson v. Kentucky*, 476 U. S. 79 (1986); *Edmonson v. Leesville Concrete Co.,* 500 U. S. 614 (1991); *Georgia v. McCollum*, 505 U. S. 42 (1992). In an effort to ensure that individuals who sit on juries are free of racial bias, the Court has held that the Constitution at times demands that defendants be permitted to ask questions about racial bias during *voir dire. Ham v. South Carolina*, 409 U. S. 524 (1973); *Rosales-Lopez*, 451 U. S. 182; Turner v. Murray, 476 U. S. 28 (1986).

The unmistakable principle underlying these precedents is that discrimination on the basis of race, "odious in all aspects, is especially pernicious in the administration of justice." *Rose v. Mitchell*, 443 U. S. 545, 555 (1979). The jury is to be "a criminal defendant's fundamental 'protection of life and liberty against race or color prejudice.'" *McCleskey v. Kemp*, 481 U. S. 279, 310 (1987) (quoting *Strauder, supra*, at 309). Permitting racial prejudice in the jury system damages "both the fact and the perception" of the jury's role as "a vital check against the wrongful exercise of power by the State." *Powers v. Ohio*, 499 U. S. 400, 411 (1991); cf. *Aldridge v. United States*, 283 U. S. 308, 315 (1931); *Buck v. Davis, ante*, at 22.

IV

A

This case lies at the intersection of the Court's decisions endorsing the no-impeachment rule and its decisions seeking to eliminate racial bias in the jury system. The two lines of precedent, however, need not conflict.

Racial bias of the kind alleged in this case differs in critical ways from the compromise verdict in *McDonald*, the drug and alcohol abuse in *Tanner*, or the pro- defendant bias in *Warger*. The behavior in those cases is troubling and unacceptable, but each involved anomalous behavior from a single jury—or juror—gone off course. Jurors are presumed to follow their oath, cf. *Penry v. Johnson*, 532 U. S. 782, 799 (2001), and neither history nor common experience show that the jury system is rife with mischief of these or similar kinds. To attempt to rid the jury of every irregularity of this sort would be to ex pose it to unrelenting scrutiny. "It is not at all clear . . . that the jury system could survive such efforts to perfect it." *Tanner*, 483 U. S., at 120.

The same cannot be said about racial bias, a familiar and recurring evil that, if left unaddressed, would risk systemic injury to the administration of justice. This Court's decisions demonstrate that racial bias implicates unique historical, constitutional, and institutional concerns. An effort to address the most grave and serious statements of racial bias is not an effort to perfect the jury but to ensure that our legal system remains capable of coming ever closer to the promise of equal treatment under the law that is so central to a functioning democracy.

Racial bias is distinct in a pragmatic sense as well. In past cases this Court has relied on other safeguards to protect the right to an impartial jury. Some of those safe guards, to be sure, can disclose racial bias. *Voir dire* at the outset of trial, observation of juror demeanor and conduct during trial, juror reports before the verdict, and nonjuror evidence after trial are important mechanisms for discovering bias. Yet their operation may be compromised, or they may prove insufficient. For instance, this Court has noted the dilemma faced by trial court judges and counsel in deciding whether to explore potential racial bias at *voir dire*. See *Rosales-Lopez, supra*; *Ristaino v. Ross*, 424 U. S. 589 (1976). Generic questions about juror impartiality may not expose specific attitudes or biases that can poison jury deliberations. Yet more pointed questions "could well exacerbate whatever prejudice might exist without substantially aiding in exposing it." *Rosales- Lopez, supra*, at 195 (Rehnquist, J., concurring in result).

The stigma that attends racial bias may make it difficult for a juror to report inappropriate statements during the course of juror deliberations. It is one thing to accuse a fellow juror of having a personal experience that improperly influences her consideration of the case, as would have been required in *Warger*. It is quite another to call her a bigot.

The recognition that certain of the *Tanner* safeguards may be less effective in rooting out racial bias than other kinds of bias is not dispositive. All forms of improper bias pose challenges to the trial process. But there is a sound basis to treat racial bias with added precaution. A constitutional rule that racial bias in the justice system must be addressed—including, in some instances, after the verdict has been entered—is necessary to prevent a systemic loss of confidence in jury verdicts, a confidence that is a central premise of the Sixth Amendment trial right.

B

For the reasons explained above, the Court now holds that where a juror makes a clear statement that indicates he or she relied on racial stereotypes or animus to convict a criminal defendant, the Sixth Amendment requires that the no-impeachment rule give way in order to permit the trial court to consider the evidence of the juror's statement and any resulting denial of the jury trial guarantee.

Not every offhand comment indicating racial bias or hostility will justify setting aside the no-impeachment bar to allow further judicial inquiry. For the inquiry to proceed, there must be a showing that one or more jurors made statements exhibiting overt racial bias that cast serious doubt on the fairness and impartiality of the jury's deliberations and resulting verdict. To qualify, the statement must tend to show that racial animus was a significant motivating factor in the juror's vote to convict. Whether that threshold showing has been satisfied is a matter committed to the substantial discretion of the trial court in light of all the circumstances, including the content and timing of the alleged statements and the reliability of the proffered evidence.

The practical mechanics of acquiring and presenting such evidence will no doubt be shaped and guided by state rules of professional ethics and local court rules, both of which often limit counsel's post-trial contact with jurors. See 27 C. Wright & V. Gold, Federal Practice and Procedure: Evidence §6076, pp. 580–583 (2d ed. 2007) (Wright); see also Variations of ABA Model Rules of Professional Conduct, Rule 3.5 (Sept. 15, 2016) (overview of state ethics rules); 2 Jurywork Systematic Techniques §13:18 (2016–2017) (overview of Federal District Court rules). These limits seek to provide jurors some protection when they return to their daily affairs after the verdict has been entered. But while a juror can always tell counsel they do not wish to discuss the case, jurors in some instances may come forward of their own accord.

That is what happened here. In this case the alleged statements by a juror were egregious and unmistakable in their reliance on racial bias. Not only did juror H. C. deploy a dangerous racial stereotype to conclude petitioner was guilty and his alibi witness should not be believed, but he also encouraged other jurors to join him in convicting on that basis.

Petitioner's counsel did not seek out the two jurors' allegations of racial bias. Pursuant to Colorado's mandatory jury instruction, the trial court had set limits on juror contact and encouraged jurors to inform the court if any one harassed them about their role in the case. Similar limits on juror contact can be found in other jurisdictions that recognize a racial-bias exception. See, *e.g.,* Fla. Standard Jury Instrs. in Crim. Cases No. 4.2 (West 2016) ("Although you are at liberty to speak with anyone about your deliberations, you are also at liberty to refuse to speak to anyone"); Mass. Office of Jury Comm'r, Trial Juror's Handbook (Dec. 2015) ("You are not required to speak with anyone once the trial is over. . . . If anyone tries to learn this confidential information from you, or if you feel harassed or embarrassed in any way, you should report it to the court . . . immediately"); N. J. Crim. Model Jury Charges, Non 2C Charges, Dismissal of Jury (2014) ("It will be up to each of you to decide whether to speak about your service as a juror").

With the understanding that they were under no obligation to speak out, the jurors approached petitioner's counsel, within a short time after the verdict, to relay their concerns about H. C.'s statements. App. 77. A similar pattern is common in cases involving juror allegations of racial bias. See, *e.g., Villar*, 586 F. 3d, at 78 (juror e mailed defense counsel within hours of the verdict); *Kittle v. United States*, 65 A. 3d 1144, 1147 (D. C. 2013) (juror wrote a letter to the judge the same day the court dis charged the jury); *Benally*, 546 F. 3d, at 1231 (juror approached defense counsel the day after the jury announced its verdict). Pursuant to local court rules, petitioner's counsel then sought and received permission from the court to contact the two jurors and obtain affidavits limited to recounting the exact statements made by H. C. that exhibited racial bias.

While the trial court concluded that Colorado's Rule 606(b) did not permit it even to consider the resulting affidavits, the Court's holding today removes that bar. When jurors disclose an instance of racial bias as serious as the one involved in this case, the law must not wholly disregard its occurrence.

1. In *Peña-Rodriguez v. Colorado*, the Supreme Court decided that juries should be safeguarded against racist and discriminatory jurists. That means that now, if a juror expresses discriminatory ideas during deliberation, they can be questioned about those statements and the findings of the jury could be overturned and the case sent back to trial in order to provide the defendant a fair trial. How do you think this ruling will impact society going forward?

2. Prior to this ruling, jurors were prohibited from discussing or testifying about deliberations that occurred after the close of a trial. Do you think that this new rule will help make sure citizens get fair, unbiased trials in the future, or will this keep jurors from being open and honest about why they're choosing to vote one way or another?

"DEAF OR BLIND PEOPLE CAN'T SERVE ON JURIES – HERE'S WHY LAW NEEDS TO CHANGE," BY JEMINA NAPIER, FROM *THE CONVERSATION* WITH THE PARTNERSHIP OF HERIOT WATT UNIVERSITY, OCTOBER 24, 2016

You might have thought any ordinary person of sound mind can serve on a jury, but actually no. Various groups are excluded in many countries including the UK, Ireland and Australia because of legal prohibitions. In the UK and Ireland, for example, deaf people are deemed "incapable" of serving as jurors if they need an interpreter, since interpreters are not permitted in the jury room. Blind people, meanwhile, are usually excluded at the judge's discretion because they can't read the court materials.

The law for both groups is similar in Australia and was recently confirmed by a final appeal decision in the Australian High Court regarding a deaf woman named Gaye Lyons who needs an interpreter even though she can read lips. She took legal action after she had been excluded from serving on a jury in Queensland in 2012.

In a decision that will potentially influence courts in the UK and other jurisdictions, the court held that Ms Lyons had not been discriminated against. It said the problem was in fact a lack of legislative provision for deaf people and could therefore only be addressed by politicians.

WHAT IS EVIDENT

Lyons' case is now being referred by the activist group People With Disability Australia to the UN Committee to the Convention on the Rights of Persons with Disabilities. The UN committee already condemned two other legal decisions earlier this year to exclude deaf people from juries in New South Wales in Australia in 2012. Meanwhile, the British Deaf Association has been actively lobbying for deaf people to serve as jurors in the UK.

As things stand, however, it looks like this strange situation is more likely to be changed by politicians than judges – whether in Australia or the UK. As one of the people spearheading research into deaf jurors, there is certainly plenty of evidence as to why it should change. I am not aware of any equivalent work into blind people but some of the same observations would almost certainly be applicable.

For deaf jurors, there's no comprehension issue. I helped establish that legal facts and concepts can be conveyed in sign language effectively enough for deaf people to access court proceedings and legal texts as well as hearing people. Deaf jurors will misunderstand certain terms and concepts, but no more than anyone else.

A survey of legal professionals and sign language interpreters from various countries in 2013 subsequently found that those in jurisdictions that already allowed deaf jurors tended to be more comfortable with having them. Having said that, respondents didn't have a problem with deaf jurors in principle and thought they could serve successfully as long as there were clear supportive policies and guidelines and training for interpreters and court staff.

A final study in which I have been involved—which is not yet published—explored a simulated trial involving a deaf juror with interpreters in Australia. The deaf juror participated effectively and was a key contributor in the deliberations. The other hearing jurors overwhelmingly said they weren't aware of the interpreters being engaged in the process or airing their opinions about the case. They saw them as neutral and not affecting the deliberation process.

In feedback sessions earlier this year, judges, lawyers, jury managers and people from deaf organisations agreed the evidence shows there is no social or linguistic impediment to deaf jurors in principle. The legal professionals did believe that the right to a fair trial should override the right to do your civic duty as a juror. They said that providing interpreters would be complex, but was achievable with careful planning. The increasing use of video conference technology was specifically mentioned as a way to provide access to interpreters more easily.

Overall, the evidence strongly suggests that deaf people should be able to serve as jurors – and it is hard to imagine any good reasons not to extend blind people the same rights. It's time the law was changed in the UK, Ireland and Australia to make this possible. Other countries already permit these kinds of people to serve, including New Zealand and most US states.

The governments and law reform commissions in the UK, Ireland and Australia are all considering this issue at present: it's high time they took it forward.

1. Deaf and blind people are frequently prohibited from serving on juries in places like the UK, Ireland, and Australia. In Australia, a woman sued for her right to be put on a jury, but the courts decided it was legal to exclude her. Do you think an exclusion like this is acceptable, or are deaf and blind citizens being further marginalized by not being allowed to serve on juries like their peers?

2. If deaf and blind citizens can't serve on juries, that means that deaf and blind defendants can't be judged by a true jury of their peers. Do you think this is something that should be considered when deciding whether they can be jurors? Do the courts have the responsibility of adapting to deaf and blind jurors, or should potential jurors who are deaf or blind have to work within the existing system?

CHAPTER 4

WHAT ADVOCACY ORGANIZATIONS SAY

Advocacy organizations have long been the leaders for social justice. As you'd expect, advocacy groups work to promote social justice, but there are hundreds, if not thousands, of groups, and each chooses to approach inequality from a different angle and with a different cure. Some promote governmental intervention and new rules and regulations to treat societal inequality. Others believe that social change begins with individuals and that, as Speaker Ryan suggested earlier in this book, private organizations are the key to social justice. As you'll see from the following articles, the issues that these advocacy groups work in are incredibly diverse, and many of the issues are intertwined, which means that even as improvements are made to some issues, new problems are likely to spring up.

"PRO-LEGALIZATION GROUPS PREPARE FOR MARIJUANA MEASURES IN 2016," BY BRIANNA GURCIULLO, KAREN MAWDSLEY, AND KATIE CAMPBELL, FROM *NEWS21*, AUGUST 15, 2015

WASHINGTON, D.C. – Advocacy groups have poured millions of dollars into legalizing both recreational and medical marijuana in states across the country.

One of the most powerful and influential groups – Washington, D.C.-based Marijuana Policy Project – was behind successful recreational measures in Alaska and Colorado, two of four states that now allow recreational use. MPP organizers hope to replicate those efforts in five other states during the 2016 elections, an undertaking they say will—if successful—prove significant for the effort to end marijuana prohibition.

One of them, Arizona, is a state that conservative icon Barry Goldwater called home. It frequently makes national headlines for controversial measures on immigration and gay rights. Voters passed the state's medical marijuana program by the barest of margins in 2010.

"Out of the five campaigns that we're running nationwide, Arizona's definitely going to be the most heated, the most active," said Carlos Alfaro, the Arizona political director for the Marijuana Policy Project. He plans to win voters by inundating the airwaves, unveiling billboards, organizing rallies and hosting debates.

It's all part of the well-funded, well-organized machine that's driving the effort toward ending prohibition nationwide. Proponents have found so much success because they have learned how to secure financial backing, take advantage of changing attitudes and address fears about legalization. The Marijuana Policy Project aims to add California, Nevada, Massachusetts and Maine to its portfolio of ballot initiative successes in 2016, along with Arizona.

Legalization efforts – many backed by other groups – could appear on the ballot in about a dozen states next year. Twenty-three states and Washington, D.C., already allow for medical marijuana use. Four states – Washington and Oregon, in addition to Colorado and Alaska – and the District of Columbia allow adults to smoke pot recreationally.

In Congress, lawmakers have started to take positions on pot and more have supported state medical marijuana laws. Both Democratic and Republican presidential candidates are talking about how they would deal with marijuana if elected. Sen. Rand Paul, R-Ky., has even courted the legal marijuana industry for campaign donations.

Leaders in the pro-legalization movement said the question is no longer whether the federal government will treat marijuana like alcohol—but when. They say the question is no longer whether the states will legalize, regulate and tax marijuana sales – but how.

"I think we're past the tipping point," said Keith Stroup, the founder of the National Organization for the Reform of Marijuana Laws, another major player in the pro-legalization effort. "There are all kinds of signs that people have figured out that prohibition is coming to an end. They may not be thrilled about it, they may not be a cheerleader for it, but when they recognize that, they begin to say, 'OK, if we're going to legalize marijuana, how do we do it in a responsible manner?'"

But legalization opponents don't plan to concede any time soon.

"I don't think that legalization is inevitable," said Alan Shinn, the executive director of the Coalition for a Drug-Free Hawaii. "The pro-marijuana people will say that it's just a matter of time before marijuana is legalized. I think there's other alternatives to legalization. We should really be taking a public health approach to this, especially with our youth."

And that's still a sticking point. The federal government classifies marijuana as one of the most dangerous drugs, "with no currently accepted medical use and a high potential for abuse," according to the Drug Enforcement Administration.

The disparity between states that have liberalized their marijuana laws and the decades-old federal prohibition of its sale and use has caused confusion in law enforcement and tension in the business world. Pro-legalization groups said that's their ultimate goal: Put so much pressure on the federal government by legalizing state by state that they can finally end the discrepancy.

"I actually consider 2016 to be what I call the game-over year because there's a good chance that a bunch of states will legalize marijuana," said Bill Piper, the director of the Drug Policy Alliance's office of national affairs. "We're reaching the point where the federal government is going to have no other choice than to change with the times."

STRATEGIC WITH RESOURCES

Advocacy groups have led ballot initiatives across the country, lobbied state legislatures and tried to convince members of Congress that leaving marijuana regulation to the states makes sense.

In the 1970s, NORML led the fight for marijuana law reform. Now, two other national organizations help run multimillion-dollar campaigns and station staff members across the country to support state measures that allow medical marijuana, decriminalize possession of small amounts of the drug or fully legalize adult use.

The Marijuana Policy Project, founded by former NORML staffers in 1995, has emerged as a political powerhouse with its robust fundraising, effective campaign messaging and expertise in drafting ballot initiatives and legislation. The Drug Policy Alliance was founded in 2000 to end the "War on Drugs." The group claims that marijuana arrests disproportionately impact racial minorities and drain law enforcement resources.

The groups and their state-level campaigns have benefited from billionaire philanthropists like Peter Lewis, the head of Progressive Insurance who died in 2013, and George Soros, the founder of Soros Fund Management. Both have donated millions of dollars to changing drug laws across the nation over the last 20 years.

During that time, the groups have honed their strategies.

Mason Tvert, director of communications for the MPP, said his organization targets states based on their history with marijuana law reform, the makeup of the state legislature, the governor's position and the level of support from local advocacy groups.

And they must carefully decide where to put their money and resources.

When Rob Kampia, the group's executive director, spoke at a National Cannabis Industry Association policy symposium in Washington, D.C., in April, he called efforts to legalize marijuana in Michigan, Missouri and Ohio "outlier initiatives" because they're less likely to pass. He said in particular, the campaign to legalize marijuana in Ohio this fall was "premature."

A MESSAGE THAT'S WORKED

Allen St. Pierre, who succeeded Stroup as executive director of NORML a decade ago, said advocates for marijuana law reform have drawn from the tactics of the social movements for women's rights, civil rights and gay rights.

"We're not trying to hardly do anything different than those groups did," St. Pierre said. "We organized. We petitioned our government peacefully for grievances. We went to the courts and asked for relief. We've used science and language to cajole, persuade and effectively win what is called in the military a 'hearts and minds' campaign."

But it hasn't been easy.

The MPP's Tvert, who was a co-director of the campaign to legalize marijuana in Colorado, said that while the public had become more accepting of medical marijuana and supportive of removing criminal penalties for using the drug, there was still "this fear surrounding marijuana for fun." Several ballot measures to legalize recreational use failed between 2002 and 2010.

At that time, Tvert said, activists had tried to sell one main message to voters: Marijuana prohibition is a government failure that forces marijuana into the black market, contributing to drug trafficking and violence. They argued that a legal market would allow for more control and would generate tax revenue.

That didn't cut it.

"That just wasn't enough," Tvert said. "Ultimately, people were still not OK with it because they just thought it was too dangerous of a substance. You can tax anything. You can tax murder for hire. Doesn't mean that people are going to think it should be legal. They think it's not good for society."

Survey results inspired legalization advocates to change tactics: Several MPP polls indicated that people were more likely to support marijuana legalization if they thought pot was less harmful than alcohol. And that became the argument behind the campaign supporting Colorado's measure to legalize recreational marijuana, Amendment 64, which passed in 2012 with 55 percent of the vote.

Colorado became a model for the MPP's efforts in other states, which have all taken the campaign name "Regulate Marijuana Like Alcohol." And the lawyer who wrote Colorado's initiative also helped draft a proposed ballot measure in Maine, said David Boyer, the group's political director for the state.

But the Maine campaign also made tweaks to its initiative, like lowering the tax rate, to make it more appealing to voters there.

BATTLING WITH LOCAL CAMPAIGNS

Different groups advocate for legalization throughout the country, and they don't always agree on the methods or details. In fact, some local groups have started to view the MPP as an unwelcome outsider.

In Maine, the organization's proposal competes with one backed by a local group, Legalize Maine. Both would legalize marijuana possession for those at least 21 years old and would allow home growing. But the two campaigns have failed to compromise on several differences.

Legalize Maine's proposal would put the state's Department of Agriculture, Conservation and Forestry in charge of regulation, while the Marijuana Policy Project's would make the Bureau of Alcoholic Beverages and Lottery Operations responsible.

Paul McCarrier, the president of Legalize Maine's board of directors, said the two groups tried to negotiate for three months. But McCarrier said MPP's initiative did not focus enough on farmers.

"I think that they're looking at Maine as just another notch in their belt that will help push their national agenda," McCarrier said. "While the Marijuana Policy Project has done a really good job at starting a conversation about marijuana legalization here in Maine and trying to push the ball around the field nationally, when it comes to marijuana legalization, they are completely out of touch with normal Mainers."

FALLING DOMINOES

Stroup said liberalization of marijuana laws has followed a general trajectory. The Western states lead the way – reducing penalties for marijuana possession, allowing residents to use medical marijuana, or eliminating all penalties for marijuana use and creating systems for regulating pot sales. Then momentum builds on the East Coast. Progress is slower in the Midwest, and movement in the South has proven most difficult.

The increase in medical marijuana programs across the country has helped to overcome the stigma surrounding marijuana, Stroup said. More than three-quarters of people support medical marijuana use, according to a 2014 National Public Radio-Truven Health Analytics poll. But only 43 percent support legalization for recreational purposes.

MPP prefers to run ballot-initiative campaigns as opposed to pushing bills through state legislatures.

But Stroup identified the legalization movement's next big turning point: Build enough political support to push the first full legalization measure through a state legislature. It's an important step because only about half of the states allow citizen-initiated ballot measures.

"We have to just simply work it every year, every chance we get, bringing in good witnesses, provide elected officials with the best information, and over a period of time, as they become more comfortable with the concept, then we'll be winning it with state legislatures," Stroup said.

But legislative measures have drawbacks as well.

"The version of legalization we win through legislatures will necessarily be more restrictive than the versions we win by voter initiatives because with an initiative, you don't have to compromise," Stroup said.

Tvert said that in 2016, Rhode Island and Vermont could become the first states to legalize marijuana through their state legislatures. A majority in both states support legalization, according to internal and independent polls conducted this year. Both state legislatures adjourned this year before acting on bills to legalize and regulate pot.

PUBLIC OPINION ON THE MOVEMENT'S SIDE

Time could be the legalization movement's greatest ally. Sixty-four percent of those between 18 and 34 years old say they support legalization, compared to 41 percent among those 55 and older, according to Gallup.

"Demographically, we knew years ago we were going to win this because young people were on our side," Stroup said. "We used to laugh, in fact, that if necessary we had a fallback strategy. And that was we would outlive our opponents. Well, I think to some degree that's exactly what we've done."

But advocates still need to convince a significant number of Americans to support recreational legalization.

"Despite the fact that the polls make it seem like it's really split down the middle, there is a huge group of people who are kind of fishy on it," said Sarah Trumble, senior policy counsel at Third Way, a centrist think tank in Washington, D.C.

Third Way refers to this group as the "marijuana middle." Many in this group support legalizing marijuana for medical use but not for recreational use.

"On this issue, like all others, values are really what drive them," said Trumble, who specializes in reaching moderates on social issues. "There's a compassion value that ties into medical marijuana, and that's why so many people support medical marijuana."

She said she expects that as more states legalize, more Americans admit that they have used marijuana and the drug becomes less stigmatized, public opinion will continue to shift toward legalization.

"We're going to have to see really how those ballot

initiatives go because if you run strong campaigns and pass laws and states do a good job of regulating marijuana, that will be the first stepping stone to other states having it," Trumble said. "But if a state, for example California, passes marijuana legalization for recreational and then does a poor job of regulating it, that could really set everything back."

LETTING THE STATES EXPERIMENT

NORML's Stroup said he hopes the Obama administration will remove marijuana from the federal government's list of the most dangerous drugs. Marijuana is listed as a Schedule I substance, which means it is a drug "with no currently accepted medical use and a high potential for abuse." Other Schedule I drugs include heroin, LSD and Ecstasy.

Stroup said he'd like to soon see marijuana reclassified as a Schedule II or Schedule III drug, which wouldn't make it legal to possess, sell or grow, but would make it easier for researchers to access. Other advocates have called for removing marijuana from the scheduling system completely.

The president has spoken about using marijuana himself as a young man, and he has said he does not believe marijuana is more dangerous than alcohol. He's recently focused on criminal justice reform, calling for shorter sentences for nonviolent drug crimes.

"At a certain point, if enough states end up decriminalizing, then Congress may then reschedule marijuana," Obama said during an interview with Vice in March. "But I always say to folks, legalization or decriminalization is not a panacea."

A 2013 Justice Department memo stated that the

federal government would only interfere under certain circumstances: if state or local law enforcement failed to prevent distribution of marijuana to minors, revenue from marijuana sales went to gangs or marijuana crossed into states where it remains illegal.

While Obama's administration hasn't interfered in states that have legalized, a future president could. That's why Stroup wants federal law to leave marijuana regulation to the states, "so it doesn't matter who's president. States are free to experiment."

Mario Moreno Zepeda, a spokesman for the Office of National Drug Control Policy, said the White House remains "committed to treating drug use as a public health issue, not just a criminal justice problem. The federal government opposes drug legalization because it runs counter to a public health and safety approach to drug policy."

"This administration's position on enforcement has been consistent: While the prosecution of drug traffickers remains an important priority, targeting individual marijuana users—especially those with serious illnesses and their caregivers—is not the best allocation of limited federal law enforcement resources," Zepeda said.

FROM 'UNTHINKABLE' TO 'MAINSTREAM'

Michael Correia, the director of government relations for the trade group National Cannabis Industry Association, said that years ago, members of Congress took no positions at all on marijuana. Now, they are beginning to support research and allowing state medical programs to continue operating.

Still, he said marijuana issues haven't become a major

priority in Congress, especially among the leadership.

"Marijuana is not global warming. It's not abortion. It's not guns. So it's not really high up on their radar screen, but it is an intriguing issue, and people need to get educated on some of the issues before they can form an opinion," Correia said.

Dan Riffle joined the MPP in 2009, and worked as a state legislative analyst for three and a half years. Now the group's director of federal policies, he said that in Congress, marijuana "is an issue that's gone from being an untouchable, unthinkable, third-rail issue to a legitimate, mainstream topic of debate."

"It's gone from a place where we struggled to have (Congress members and staffers) take meetings with us, to have our phone calls returned, to now people reach out to us and ask us to come in and brief them and use us as a resource," Riffle said.

Riffle tailors his message to his audience. If he meets with a member of the Congressional Black Caucus, for example, Riffle talks about the disparity in arrests between blacks and whites. If he sits down with a Republican who has libertarian tendencies, he drives home the argument that smoking pot is an individual decision.

Riffle said Congress is grappling with federal law that prohibits marijuana and state laws that allow its use. He said some lawmakers have tried to "address symptoms of that disease" with bills that would allow marijuana businesses to use banks, or permit Veterans Affairs doctors to recommend medical marijuana for veterans who live in states where it's legal.

"But then you're going to have other folks who say, 'Look, rather than passing seven, eight, 12 different bills depending on what the issue is, let's just grapple with the underlying problem,' which is the conflict between state and federal marijuana laws," Riffle said.

The Respect State Marijuana Laws Act – introduced by Rep. Dana Rohrabacher, R-Calif. – would do that by amending the Controlled Substances Act. It would change the federal law to protect anyone producing, possessing, distributing, dispensing, administering or delivering marijuana in states where those actions are legal. The bill has 14 co-sponsors, including six Republicans.

Rep. Earl Blumenauer, D-Ore., a longtime champion of marijuana law reform, said he anticipates the federal government will treat marijuana like alcohol within a decade.

"My judgment is with a new administration, with several more states legalizing, with public opinion solidifying, and with more and better research, I think in the next administration and the next Congress or two, we'll be in a position to just basically say, 'States, do what you want to do,'" Blumenauer said.

News21 reporter Anne M. Shearer contributed to this article.

1. The authors of the article above discuss how legalizing marijuana could help cut down on the number of drug offenders locked up or otherwise put through the criminal justice system for non-violent offenses, which inordinately affects black citizens compared to whites. Do you think that this argument makes legalization of marijuana a social justice issue?

2. Advocates for legalization also discuss how legalization would make it easier for people who need medical marijuana but don't live in states where that has been made legal yet. Do you think that focusing on the medical issue makes marijuana a social justice issue? If so, who do you think counts as the marginalized class here? If not, why not?

"WHEN DEALING WITH THE POLICE, DEAF PEOPLE ARE AT A MAJOR DISADVANTAGE," BY JEMINA NAPIER, FROM *THE CONVERSATION* WITH THE PARTNERSHIP OF HERIOT WATT, AUGUST 3, 2016

We all have occasions when we need to deal with the police. Perhaps your car has been stolen and you have to report it; or perhaps you have witnessed a mugging and you have been called to the police station to be interviewed and provide a witness statement. Or perhaps you have been accused of shoplifting and the security guard has detained you in the back room until the police arrive.

Interacting with the police can be stressful, regardless of whether you are a witness, a victim or a culprit. Most of us have one very useful advantage, however: we can hear. Anyone who is deaf and has dealt with the police may have found communication a major problem. Too often, the forces in the UK and elsewhere in Europe struggle to provide sign language interpreters at short notice or even to understand the needs of deaf people. It hampers their access to justice and needs to be addressed urgently.

The first thing to make clear is that we are talking about quite a substantial number of people. The European Union of the Deaf estimates there are approximately a million deaf sign language users in Europe. In the UK, there are estimated to be approximately 70,000 deaf people who use British Sign Language as their first or preferred language.

This is a linguistic and cultural minority group with its own accepted norms of behaviour. And most people probably don't realise that deaf people use different sign languages in every country around the world. They identify one another on that basis in the same way that a British person might identify a German or Spaniard through the way they talk.

INTERPRETER RIGHTS

When it comes to the justice system as a whole, deaf people's right to interpreters has increasingly been recognised – even if this is typically enshrined in disability discrimination law rather than laws to protect cultural minorities. But while there are now established systems for providing interpreters in courts and tribunals, and clear guidelines on booking them for police interviews and solicitor consultations in the UK and some other countries across Europe, researchers have repeatedly found that deaf people encounter barriers.

The issues are often to do with people in the justice system not being aware of the need to book interpreters to ensure that deaf people can communicate. This can usually be resolved in time for court cases or for courses in prison, but what happens in police encounters at short notice?

There are reports of police misreading a deaf person's attempts to communicate. On some occasions, deaf people have had to wait many hours before an interpreter can be found and they can be interviewed by police.

There are recurring cases of people giving witness statements without an interpreter (or with an unqualified person). The statement is then admitted as evidence in court, and the deaf person doesn't understand the process they have been involved in or the consequences of signing the statement. As the police interview is the first point of contact in a legal process, it is essential that people understand their rights and the process. This can't happen for deaf people if they don't have a professional qualified interpreter in the interview.

JUSTISIGNS

To better understand the problem in police settings and address the barriers, I have been collaborating with a team of international specialists for the past three years. The JUSTISIGNS project includes seven universities and sign language professional bodies from the UK, Switzerland, Belgium and Ireland.

We found that there is no uniform approach across Europe to training or certifying legal sign language interpreters or making such people available for deaf people in the justice system. Through a series of focus groups and interviews with police officers, deaf people and interpreters in the four countries, our findings included:

- Police officers are unaware that sign-language users need to have an interpreter present as they cannot necessarily lipread or write notes; and are unclear on the qualifications or level of expertise required of sign language interpreters. There are no clear guidelines for how interpreters and police can work together;

- Some police forces have policies to guide officers when it comes to interviewing deaf suspects/witnesses/victims – in the UK, some forces have begun to develop online videos for example – but police officers do not always know about best practice;

- There are not enough interpreters available at short notice to meet recommendations that only qualified and experienced practitioners be used in the legal system;

- Though some interpreters have received legal training, interpreters are often nervous of working in police interviews in case they get called as a witness in a later court case;

- There is a lack of established legal terminology in British Sign Language and other sign languages.

On the back of this evidence, JUSTISIGNS held masterclasses and training workshops for police officers and interpreters in the partner countries; and events and meetings to inform deaf people and other relevant organisations and professionals of the project. In the UK, it helped develop best practice guidelines on legal interpreting and worked with Police Scotland on a British Sign Language translation of the Scottish law caution and an explanation of what it means.

The hope is that in years to come, deaf people will be able to deal with the police in unexpected situations without any disadvantage. That is certainly what they are entitled to expect.

1. Because deaf people don't communicate verbally and can't hear what's being said, they often have difficulties in interactions with the police, as the author discusses. Since in most instances it is unlikely that the police know they are dealing with a deaf person at the start of the interaction, what are some steps you think should be taken to make sure that deaf and hard-of-hearing citizens receive the same treatment as their hearing counterparts?

2. Deafness is often treated as a disability instead of a separate culture, although many deaf people feel that they should be treated as a unique culture with a unique language—like people from another country who speak a foreign language. Do you think that treating deaf citizens as a different culture instead of a disabled group would help them in their fight for equality, or hurt them?

"URBAN FOOD DESERTS THREATEN CHILDREN'S HEALTH," BY MARIAN WRIGHT EDELMAN, FROM *OTHERWORDS*, JANUARY 11, 2010

ACCESS TO NUTRITIOUS FOOD IS A MATTER OF SOCIAL JUSTICE

Anybody forced to live in a desert would find survival in a barren, desolate wasteland difficult. But through a series of public policies and private-sector decisions, millions of mostly low-income and minority families in America have been condemned to subsist in vast urban "food deserts" that pose serious health threats to their children.

Food deserts, areas with no or distant grocery stores, are communities where residents can buy food only at "convenience" stores, liquor stores, gas stations, or fast-food restaurants that sell foods high in fat, sugar, and salt. Getting to stores that offer a greater variety of foods is often challenging to families without cars, especially when many city and state governments have cut back on public transportation. While many Americans are resolving to eat more healthfully, children and families living in "food deserts" lack that choice.

The health and vitality of people living in many urban neighborhoods can differ from block to block, depending on how near they are to a grocery store offering reasonably priced fresh fruits and vegetables. In many urban neighborhoods it's easier to buy a pint of liquor, a fried chicken wing, or a gun than a fresh tomato. The failure of supermarket chains to locate stores with fresh produce to inner-city communities—a form of food redlining—has a profound impact on the nutrition of families lacking cars or access to public transportation.

Tragically, children in families trapped in food-desert zip codes risk becoming obese and developing early hypertension and full-blown high blood pressure, which can lead to Type 2 diabetes and heart disease.

Food deserts originated with the urban "white flight" of the 1960s and 1970s. According to PolicyLink, a national nonprofit focused on social and economic inequities, when white, middle-class residents left cities for the suburbs, grocery stores followed. In urban communities from Los Angeles to Washington, D.C., and from Detroit to Houston, the nearest grocery store is twice as far as the nearest fast-food restaurant. About 400,000 Chicago residents live in areas with nearby fast-food restaurants, but no or distant grocery stores.

A 2003 University of Michigan study found only five grocery stores larger than 20,000 square feet in Detroit. And while 24 percent of Washington, D.C.'s population lives in the predominantly black areas east of the Anacostia River, only 15 percent of the city's 360 food stores are there.

Nationally, typical low-income neighborhoods have 30 percent fewer supermarkets than higher-income neighborhoods. The problem isn't only in urban areas; food deserts are also common in many rural communities. Across the country, too many families are forced to do their food shopping in convenience stores stocked with overpriced, highly processed, fatty food with low nutritional value, often past its expiration date. In stores like these, staples such as milk can cost more than at supermarkets.

It's good to know that a number of groups are addressing this problem. The Philadelphia-based nonprofit organization Food Trust is working with schools to provide healthy food and offering corner stores financing to stock healthy food and upgrade their refrigeration systems to better preserve fruits and vegetables. Various organizations are seeking federal and local anti-obesity funding to replicate this effort. Such programs can make a real difference. In a 2002 study, University of North Carolina researchers found African Americans ate an average of 32 percent more fruits and vegetables for each supermarket in their census tract.

Access to nutritious food is a matter of social justice. We must follow the lead of First Lady Michelle Obama, whose community garden at the White House has focused public attention on better nutrition as part of a national movement, to improve children's health and prevent obesity and diabetes. If we fail to ensure our children receive better nutrition, our nation will pay a heavy price in increased rates of obesity, diabetes, hypertension, cardiovascular disease, and cancer, resulting in the loss of resources and productivity. As legislators struggle to reform our nation's health-care system and contain its skyrocketing costs, addressing the problem of access to nutritious food is an obvious step.

Marian Wright Edelman is president of the Children's Defense Fund.

1. The author of this article discusses how low-income families, already at a disadvantage, are more likely to live in a "food desert," with little access to affordable fresh foods. What are some issues that you can see stemming from having to live in a food desert?

2. The article discusses that "food deserts" began appearing when white families left the cities for the suburbs in the 1960s and 1970s, tying the issue in with not only economic inequality, but racial inequality as well. What are some other social justice matters that you can think of that have multiple causes?

"WE STILL NEED BLACK HISTORY MONTH," BY MARC MORIAL, FROM *OTHERWORDS*, FEBRUARY 3, 2016

AMERICA'S RACIAL DISPARITY WON'T DISAPPEAR IF WE SIMPLY IGNORE IT

Carter G. Woodson was born in Virginia, 10 years after the fall of the Confederacy. Working as a sharecropper and a miner, he rarely had time to attend school until the age of 20.

But he sure made up for lost time. Woodson would devote the rest of his life to studying, and today he's known as the father of African-American history.

Through his studies, Woodson wrote, he found that African-American contributions to history "were overlooked, ignored, and even suppressed by the writers of history textbooks and the teachers who use them."

He concluded that racial prejudice "is merely the logical result of tradition, the inevitable outcome of thorough instruction to the effect that the Negro has never contributed anything to the progress of mankind."

And that, he believed, had a dispiriting effect on young black people. "Those who have no record of what their forebears have accomplished lose the inspiration which comes from the teaching of biography and history," he observed.

Black History Month, which Woodson founded as Negro History Week in 1926, was his effort to combat that tradition. Chosen to coincide with the birthdays of Abraham Lincoln and Frederick Douglass, the second week in February was designated as a time to celebrate black history.

The first year, education officials in just three states and two cities recognized the event. But by 1929 it was being promoted in nearly every state in the nation.

In 1970, black students at Kent State University celebrated the first unofficial Black History Month. Just a few years later, in 1976, President Gerald Ford himself officially recognized the event. "In celebrating Black History Month," Ford said, we can make "progress in the realization of the ideals envisioned by our Founding Fathers."

And, seizing on Woodson's efforts, he added: "Even more than this, we can seize the opportunity to honor the too-often neglected accomplishments of black Americans in every area of endeavor throughout our history."

In the intervening 40 years, we've seen remarkable progress in racial justice—and also heartbreaking setbacks. These days there are some people in the black community—like actress Stacey Dash—who, as in Woodson's own day, feel Black History Month is unnecessary.

And their essential point is valid: Black history is American history, and we shouldn't relegate its teaching to one month a year. But that isn't the point of Black History Month.

The American dream remains perilously out of reach for many people of color. The National Urban League Equality Index—a figure my organization developed as a comprehensive comparison of black America's status in the areas of economics, health, education, social justice, and civic engagement—stands at just 72 percent.

That racial disparity won't disappear if we simply ignore it. Justice won't be achieved unless we actively seek it out. Black History Month not only serves as a reminder of what our forebears have achieved, but as an inspiration for the journey that remains before us.

Marc Morial is the CEO of the National Urban League.

1. The importance of Black History Month, the author says, is in showing the often-ignored contributions to society made by African Americans. Black History Month, he says, is a way of fighting for social justice

and demanding equality. What impact do you think learning about black citizens' societal contributions will have on achieving social equality? Do you think there would be a chance for racial equality if we didn't take time to learn more about other races?

2. The author says that "racial disparity won't disappear if we ignore it." What are some ways that we're making social justice issues visible today, other than through events like Black History Month? What are some ways you can think of to help people learn about social justice issues?

"TENSIONS HIGH AS COMBAT-READY POLICE CONFRONT NATIONAL BLACK LIVES MATTER PROTESTS," BY DEIDRE FULTON, FROM *COMMON DREAMS*, JULY 11, 2016

'THE RHETORIC OF THE PROTEST IN NO WAY MATCHES THE VIOLENCE THAT POLICE HAVE BEEN INFLICTING ON PEOPLE,' NOTES ACTIVIST DERAY MCKESSON

After a weekend of protests and arrests across the U.S., demonstrations against police violence continued on Sunday in cities nationwide.

As *Common Dreams* reported, marches and rallies responding to the recent fatal police shootings of Alton Sterling and Philando Castile took place Saturday in Phoenix, New York City, Washington, D.C., Indianapolis, San Francisco, Nashville, Baton Rouge, Minneapolis/St. Paul, and Rochester, New York. In St. Paul, an overnight face-off on Interstate-94 resulted in more than 100 arrests, while in Baton Rouge, nearly 200 people have been arrested since Friday.

Activist DeRay Mckesson, one of those arrested in Louisiana on Saturday, was released in the afternoon on Sunday. He spoke to CNN on Monday.

Demonstrators took to the streets Sunday for mostly peaceful rallies in Boston, Massachusetts; Charleston and Columbia, South Carolina; Memphis, Tennessee; Atlanta, Georgia; Washington, D.C., and beyond; more protests and rallies are planned for Monday.

In Baton Rouge, Louisiana, however, tensions were heightened. According to the *New Orleans Advocate*:

> What began Sunday as a peaceful march over the death of Alton Sterling turned into a standoff in downtown Baton Rouge between officers threatening to gas the crowds and protesters throwing debris at police.
>
> For at least three hours, officers and protesters were locked in an intense confrontation that occasionally erupted into skirmishes... At least 48 people were arrested.
>
> More than 100 officers circled the crowd. Many of the officers arrived holding assault rifles, and police used a high-pitched siren called an "LRAD,"

> a long-range acoustic device intended to disperse the crowd with its ear-splitting sound.
>
> Three armored vehicles accompanied officers decked out in riot gear. For the first time since the protests began last week, officers showed up with gas masks.

Such increased militarization drew criticism on social media.

In an interview with the *New Yorker* published Sunday, Black Lives Matter network co-founder Alicia Garza predicted such an outcome in the wake of last week's shootings in Dallas and urged the movement to "think bigger":

> The deaths of these officers will absolutely create the conditions for increased security, surveillance, and monitoring of protesters. It will absolutely usher in additional post-9/11-like measures that allow the state to profile people based either on their political beliefs or on their political activities, and then, of course, I think we will also probably see a push for an expansion of the police state, rather than the reduction of one.
>
> If we can anticipate that, then that means that it's no longer acceptable to fight for reforms like body cameras, and certainly I think it means that we have to think bigger. The call that I heard from many, many activists and their supporters over the last few days has been, "We can't just march and protest." There has to be something bigger than that.

Since a lone gunman shot 12 police officers in Dallas on Thursday, killing five, racial justice advocates have found themselves forced to defend their actions from those who "are using this really unfortunate incident to cast a negative light on our very important and necessary movement," as Opal Tometi, another Black Lives Matter co-founder, put it.

"That's what I'm seeing. I hope it does not cause consequences for us," Tometi said. "What I'm seeing right now is that there is an extra amount of attention that's being placed on folks who are doing their civic duty and are protesting and are exercising their rights, and I'm concerned that there might be some efforts that are going to be used to stop that very important expression of their freedom of speech, and the disdain and disgust and very righteous outrage that people have. Because we've been seeing, like DeRay said, almost every day, somebody is being murdered in our nation. It is unacceptable."

With more protests and rallies on the horizon, Jamira Burley, Amnesty International USA's campaign manager for gun violence and criminal justice reform, said Sunday from Baton Rouge: "In the wake of this intensely emotional week, it is understandable that people across the country have been moved to take to the streets to peacefully exercise their right to be heard. Police have a duty to facilitate the right to peaceful protest while still protecting their own safety and that of the public."

She added: "The sheer number of arrests last night raises serious questions about proportionate response to peaceful protests. Law enforcement officers cannot selectively decide which laws to enforce during demonstrations—be it against journalists, legal observers or protestors."

1. In 2016, after the killings of unarmed black men by police, several police officers were killed, possibly in retaliation, and police responded by arming heavily while policing protests held by the Black Lives Matter advocacy group. After reading this article, as well as previous articles in this book about how protests for social justice can often lead to further issues before anything is resolved, do you think protests are the best way to fight for social justice? If not, what are other non-violent methods that you think advocacy groups could use?

2. One of the people quoted in the article raises the question of appropriate police response to peaceful protest, and how participants in the Black Lives Matter protests, as well as journalists covering the protests, were unfairly targeted. Similar statements were made during the Occupy Wall Street movement several years earlier. Do you think this problem is a symptom of social injustice, or a cause? Or both? Explain.

CHAPTER 5

WHAT THE MEDIA SAY

The media often advocate for social justice as much as advocacy organizations, particularly in pushing people in power—like politicians and government officials—to justify their actions on these matters. Investigative journalists also work to expose injustice and inequality, whether in the workforce, the government, or other areas of life. Without journalists, many of the social justice issues discussed in this book would not be as widely known or understood, and the average citizen would have little way of learning about issues that don't directly impact them. Journalists work to spread the truth about matters as diverse as climate change and the refugee crisis, but as you'll see in the following collection of articles, they also work to promote equality among their own ranks.

"WILL TRUMP'S CLIMATE TEAM ACCEPT ANY 'SOCIAL COST OF CARBON'?" BY ANDREW REVKIN, FROM *PROPUBLICA*, JANUARY 11, 2017

President-elect Donald Trump and members of his proposed cabinet and transition team have taken aim at many of President Obama's climate and clean-energy policies, programs and legacies—from the Paris Agreement to the Clean Power Plan.

But there's probably no more consequential and contentious a target for the incoming administration than an arcane metric called the "social cost of carbon."

This value is the government's best estimate of how much society gains over the long haul by cutting each ton of the heat-trapping carbon-dioxide emissions scientists have linked to global warming.

Currently set at $36 per ton of carbon dioxide, the metric is produced using a complex, and contentious, set of models estimating a host of future costs to society related to rising temperatures and seas, then using a longstanding economic tool, a discount rate, to gauge how much it is worth today to limit those harms generations hence. (For context, the United States emitted about 5.1 billion tons of CO2 in 2015, out of a global total of 36 billion.)

The contention arises because the social cost of carbon underpins justifications for policies dealing with everything from power plants to car mileage to refrigerator efficiency. The carbon valuation has already helped shape 79 regulations.

The strongest sign of a coming challenge to the social cost calculation came in a post-election memorandum from Thomas Pyle, who was then president of the industry-funded American Energy Alliance and Institute for Energy Research and who now leads the Trump transition team for the Department of Energy. In the memo, he predicted policies resulting in "ending the use of the social cost of carbon in federal rule makings."

Outright elimination of such a calculation is highly unlikely, according to interviews with a range of experts. The practice of estimating the economic costs and benefits of most government regulations began under an executive order of President Ronald Reagan in 1981. It has continued ever since. Climate-related regulations are no different. Several court rulings have affirmed the process.

But the Trump administration's aim of lowering the operative "number," possibly by a lot, is almost assured. In 2013, an economist from Pyle's energy institute testified in a Senate hearing that under a proper calculation, the social cost of carbon "would probably be close to zero, or possibly even negative."

A deep cut would be both dangerous and unjustified, given the basics of both climate science and economics, said Gernot Wagner, a Harvard economist focused on climate risk and policy. In a phone interview on Tuesday, he said the interagency working group assembled by the White House in 2009 to create the social cost measurement was "a damn impressive exercise at assembling a lot of firepower and done in a way that was about as apolitical as things can go in Washington."

The result, he said, is, if anything, far too conservative. "What worries me most, frankly, is that the current social cost is basically being portrayed as the upper limit," he said.

In fact, he and several other climate-focused economists said in interviews that the science, including persistent uncertainty on how fast temperatures and seas will rise, should result in a higher carbon cost and even more aggressive steps at limiting warming.

At the same time, he and other analysts agreed that there are issues with the way calculations have been done so far, reflected in a flood of comments received by the Office of Management and Budget in 2015.

A fresh independent assessment of ways to improve the process was just conducted by the National Academy of Sciences, the nation's leading independent scientific advisory body.

The report, "Valuing Climate Damages: Updating Estimation of the Social Cost of Carbon Dioxide," was released yesterday.

The main recommendation is to "unbundle" the mix of models behind that seemingly simple dollar figure. The models, melding climate science, demographic change and economics, project harms by looking at possible shifts in human populations, technologies, economies and the climate in coming decades.

The assumptions and uncertainties for each step could then be more clearly laid out in transparent ways that might constrain misinterpretations and boost societal, and political, acceptance.

Myles R. Allen, an author of the report and a climate scientist at Oxford University, said in an interview that such a structure could help clarify where data ends and societal and political choices begin.

"There are obviously political decisions which need to be made in any calculation like the social cost of carbon," he said. "On the other hand, the way the climate system responds to greenhouse gas emission levels is not really up for political discussion."

Here are some additional resources on the social cost of carbon and related issues:

- The most readable, even enjoyable, summary of discount rates in the context of climate change was written by David Roberts, now at Vox, back in his Grist days: "Discount rates: A boring thing you should know about (with otters!)."
- The two architects of the social cost of carbon, Michael Greenstone, who was on the White House Council of Economic Advisers early in Obama's first term, and Cass R. Sunstein, at the Office of Management and Budget, wrote a Times op-ed in December in defense of the measurement headlined "Donald Trump Should Know: This Is What Climate Change Costs Us."
- Gernot Wagner co-authored a new working paper that offers lessons from risk-management practices used in investing in cutting through debates about the present value of limiting future climate risk: "Applying Asset Pricing Theory to Calibrate the Price of Climate Risk," by Kent D. Daniel, Robert B. Litterman, and Gernot Wagner (National Bureau of Economic Research).
- Richard J. Lazarus, a Harvard law professor, wrote a paper with perhaps the most succinct and apt title in academic literature: "Super Wicked Problems and Climate Change: Restraining the Present to Liberate the Future" (first published in the Cornell Law Review, July 2009).
- I wrote a Dot Earth column on a climatologist's view of the challenge in investing now for the far future called "How the Climate Challenge Could Derail a Brilliant Human Destiny."

1. The author discusses the social cost of carbon pollution. Earlier in the book you read about how climate change—in part caused by carbon emissions—has an impact on economic and social inequality. Based on what you've just read, what do you think can be done with regard to carbon pollution to help fight this injustice?

"ALLEGED CHICAGO ASSAULT REIGNITES ISSUE OF HATE CRIMES AGAINST WHITES," BY JOE SEXTON, FROM *PROPUBLICA*, JANUARY 5, 2017

AS CHICAGO AUTHORITIES WAITED BEFORE FILING HATE-CRIME CHARGES AGAINST FOUR YOUNG ADULT BLACKS FOR AN ALLEGED ATTACK ON A WHITE DISABLED MAN, THE INTERNET RAGED.

The meaning and enforcement of the Illinois hate-crimes statute seems destined for intense scrutiny with the arrest this week of four young black adults in Chicago in connection with the assault of a mentally disabled white man. The arrests by the Chicago Police Department resulted in part from what appeared to a livestreamed video of the disabled man being abused while bound and gagged. The recording captures one or more of the attackers making references to Donald Trump and white people.

The Illinois hate-crime statute reads as follows:

> A person commits hate crime when, by reason of the actual or perceived race, color, creed, religion, ancestry, gender, sexual orientation, physical or mental disability, or national origin of another individual or group of individuals, regardless of the existence of any other motivating factor or factors, he commits assault, battery, aggravated assault, misdemeanor theft, criminal trespass to residence, misdemeanor criminal damage to property, criminal trespass to vehicle, criminal trespass to real property, mob action, disorderly conduct, harassment by telephone, or harassment through electronic communications.

On Wednesday, Commander Kevin Duffin said the department was weighing whether to bring hate-crime charges against the suspects, saying it was not yet clear whether the attack was motivated by bias, according to The Washington Post.

"They're young adults. And they make stupid decisions," Duffin was quoted saying in the Post account. "That certainly will be part of whether or not we seek a hate crime to determine whether this is sincere or just stupid ranting and raving."

On Thursday, however, CNN reported that formal hate-crime charges had indeed been filed. The arrests, as well as the police's inquiry into the circumstances of the alleged attack, set off a perhaps not surprising firestorm on social media. The police were blasted for their failure to immediately charge the accused with hate crimes. The media were criticized for supposedly failing to adequately cover the incident.

The issue of hate crimes being committed against white people has flared occasionally over the years, and last year the website Broadly explored it in a post. It noted that a black Wisconsin teen's conviction for assaulting a 14-year-old white boy under a hate-crimes statute had ultimately been upheld by the U.S. Supreme Court, and endorsed by the American Civil Liberties Union. The black teen had allegedly said "Do you feel all hyped up to move on some white people" after watching the movie "Mississippi Burning."

James Jacobs, a professor of constitutional law at New York University and the courts director for the Center for Research in Crime and Justice, told Broadly, "There's nothing unusual about applying hate crime laws to black defendants who harbor racist motivations against their victims."

ProPublica reported late last year on recent hate crimes in New York City. According to data kept by the New York Police Department, there had been 380 hate crimes reported in 2016. Crimes against Muslims were up 50 percent from the same time last year. Crimes involving sexual orientation were also up.

But whites had been victims, too—the source of 16 reported crimes, nearly double the number of the year prior and most involving acts of violence.

The subject of hate crimes—how they are defined, how they are enforced, how they are reported by the media—has only intensified since the presidential election. Many critics of Trump's campaign warned that his racially inflammatory policy positions and rhetoric would inspire violence against minorities and immigrants. Trump, for his part, has said that was not his intent. But his supporters have occasionally seized on reports of hate crimes, questioning their prevalence and veracity. The false report made by a Muslim girl in New York City was one such example.

Hate-crime data is poorly collected across the country, something ProPublica hopes to help remedy in 2017 with a yearlong project aimed at documenting and verifying bias incidents. The FBI counts between 5,000 and 10,000 hate crimes annually, though surveys by the federal Bureau of Justice indicate that there may be as many as 250,000. While the FBI's data is incomplete, anti-white crimes make up about 20 percent of recorded hate crimes annually.

Brian Levin, the director of the Center for the Study of Hate and Extremism at California State University, said that while anti-white hate crimes make up a disproportionately small number of hate crimes given the white population, they are still given too little focus. "[Anti-white crime] exists, and when it happens it does not get the same kind of moral outrage that it should," he said. But Levin said this crime should not raise questions about "one group being bad and another group being good," but should push society to face a larger problem of coarseness throughout the country.

"The more that Americans feel unmoored from the institutions and creed that holds us together, the more often this kind of crap is going to happen on all sides of the spectrum," he said, adding that minority groups that have traditionally been targeted will also act out because of this in ways that shouldn't be ignored. "The idea that a group that has faced discrimination — African Americans, Jews — is somehow inoculated against having the effects of an increasingly coarse society affect their members is an illusion."

The Southern Poverty Law Center, an advocacy organization that has long monitored hate crimes and bias incidents, has long recorded attacks against whites, and has pledged to do so going forward, including those crimes against whites possibly inspired by Trump's victory. So far the SPLC has recorded 23 anti-Trump incidents, though it acknowledges this may be an undercount given who is most likely to report incidents of bias to the SPLC.

Richard Cohen, president of the SPLC, declared the alleged Chicago assault a hate crime. "Whether this is a hate crime based on disability or a hate crime based on race, I think it is incumbent on the authorities to act swiftly," he said, calling the crime "incredibly shocking."

"The anti-white and anti-Trump remarks came one after the other," Cohen said of the recording. "I take it as a synonym for anti-white rhetoric in their minds."

The authorities, with the filing of charges Thursday, appeared for the moment to agree.

1. The article discusses, among other things, whether a hate crime can be committed against a white person—long a disputed idea because of the marginalization of other races. The author and the Supreme Court uphold that a hate crime can be committed against a person for being white, however. Do you think, as some of the experts in the article suggest, that hate crimes against whites are underreported?

2. While it is suggested that anti-white hate crimes make up 20 percent of annual hate crimes, there are many who still believe there is no such thing as an anti-white hate crime. Do you think that acknowledging anti-white crimes will help authorities fight hate crimes, or will it diminish the efforts other groups make to fight social injustice for more marginalized populations?

"BYLINE INEQUALITY MATTERS," BY EMILY SCHWARTZ GRECO, FROM *OTHERWORDS*, AUGUST 19, 2015

THE EDITORIAL SERVICE I RUN HAS GOTTEN LESS MALE BUT REMAINS TOO PALE

Anna Quindlen relayed an eye-opening and hair-raising experience to her readers in 1990.

"A newspaper editor said to me not long ago, with no hint of self-consciousness, 'I'd love to run your column, but we already run Ellen Goodman,'" the *New York Times* columnist wrote. "Not only was there a quota; there was a quota of one."

A quarter of a century later, many newspapers still have far to go. On a recent slow news day, white men wrote every bylined commentary in *The Washington Post's* op-ed pages.

Even the most well-meaning white men can't speak for the rest of us.

Granted, the *Post* regularly features the analysis of Eugene Robinson, an African-American man, and Fareed Zakaria, an immigrant born in India. It also runs Kathleen Parker and other white women. Several of the paper's Metro and Business section columnists are people of color, including at least two black women.

But that pale and male lineup that caught my eye was no blip.

While the *Post* does distribute columns written by Esther Cepeda and Ruben Navarrette, it doesn't publish work by either of them or any other people of Latin American descent in its own pages. Given that the 54 million Latinos living in the United States compose our largest minority, can't Washington's dominant news source find room for the opinions expressed by a single person from this community?

Detailed research on byline balance is clear if infrequent. A 2012 Op-Ed Project study found that male opinion-page writers still outnumber female writers four-to-one.

This leaves most op-ed sections more testosterone-laced than the subset of Donald Trump's Twitter followers who cheer when he disses Megyn Kelly.

In addition to this quantity problem, there are quality concerns. The Op-Ed Project found that a disproportionate share of women's commentaries address "pink" things like gender, food, and family, versus economics, politics, national security, and other hard-news topics.

The mainstream media's even more muffled when it comes to amplifying voices from communities of color.

The last time the media watchdog group Fairness and Accuracy In Reporting (FAIR) did the bean-counting, whites wrote up to 94 percent of the opinion pieces that ran in the three most prominent newspapers.

And like *The Washington Post, The New York Times* still doesn't publish a single Latino columnist.

How does OtherWords, the editorial service I run, measure up?

Some background: William A. Collins founded Minuteman Media in 1998 as a bulwark against the growing dominance of conservatives in the nation's opinion pages. When this avuncular former Norwalk, Connecticut mayor handed me the reins of his editorial service six years ago, most of the folks writing the commentaries we distributed were pale and male.

By 2012, women were writing a quarter of the pieces that this editorial service, by then renamed, got published in newspapers. That was better but not good enough. Today, partly because of my column, women pen half of our work.

Achieving gender equality makes our scrappy outfit stand out. But people of color wrote only 5 percent of our commentaries in the first half of this year, in line with the media's overall lack of diversity.

Working within the confines of a shoestring budget, OtherWords brings under-exposed yet bold voices to the kitchen tables of the good people from Union, South Carolina to Gardena, California — and hundreds of towns in between. Now that we're less male, can we get less pale? We can and we must.

Because byline inequality matters.

1. In her article, the author discusses the lack of diversity in the media, which she perceives as a problem. Do you think it's important that newspapers, magazines, and websites have diverse staffs, made up of people of different genders, religions, races, and ethnicities? Why do you think this matters?

2. How do you think newsroom diversity would help the media? Are there stories you think are being covered poorly—or not at all—because of the fact that many news organizations remain mostly white and male?

"JUSTICE SHOULD BE THE DRIVING FORCE FOR REPORTING ON THE REFUGEE CRISIS," BY STEVEN HARKINS, FROM *THE CONVERSATION* WITH THE PARTNERSHIP OF THE UNIVERSITY OF SHEFFIELD, SEPTEMBER 18, 2015

If truth, accuracy and objectivity guaranteed that all journalism would be ethical, the cause of the Syrian refugees would have been taken up long before the shocking images of three-year-old Aylan Kurdi's body washed up on a Turkish beach. The publication of the image triggered a brief volte-face in sections of the British press that had been blaming the victims for the refugee crisis.

Newspapers agonised over the ethical issues raised by publishing such a shocking image. In response to reader's complaints for publishing the image, Berlin-based newspaper Bild removed every image from a subsequent edition.

This will become a staple case study for journalism ethics students at universities. But it will also raise questions about how journalists are trained. Journalism education should not only be able to teach people how to do journalism but also why.

BLAMING THE REFUGEES

The way that sections of the British press have blamed the victims of the refugee crisis will receive far less attention on the ethics curriculum. Prior to the publication of the photograph refugees had been described as "freeloaders" (the Daily Express), who were "swamping" (the Sun) the UK with either "desperate families" or "chancers" (the Daily Mail).

This split between "deserving" and "undeserving" victims is a familiar trope in news coverage of vulnerable groups such as refugees and people living in poverty. Political economist Thomas Malthus argued that the population would eventually outgrow available resources, so it is a mistake to help the most vulnerable people because it would accelerate population growth.

This distinction forms part of a rationale of news reporting which focuses on scarcity of resources rather than their distribution. This passage from an article in The Telegraph in August is a good example:

> *If we submit to pressure, and open our doors further, where on Earth will those coming through them live, given the chronic shortage of housing? And where will their children go to school, given the pressure on places especially in the South East?*

If this issue was framed through the lens of social justice rather than Malthusian ideology, the reporter might have noted that in 2014 there were 11m empty houses in Europe.

In the meantime, news articles about refugees have got more extreme. Katie Hopkins, a columnist for the Sun described people trying to get to the UK as a "plague of feral humans" who were "like cockroaches." The UN High Commissioner for Human Rights complained that Hopkins used "language very similar" to the language used by the

Kangura newspaper and Radio Mille Collines prior to the 1994 Rwandan genocide.

The Independent Press Standards Organisation (IPSO) rejected complaints that the article was discriminatory. This prompted the chair of the National Union of Journalist's ethical council to say that "such language must be considered a breach of ethical codes." IPSO was set up following the 2012 Leveson Inquiry, the public inquiry into the press following the recent phone-hacking scandal, where employers and educators of the next generation of journalists emphasised their commitment to high ethical standards.

ETHICAL FRAMEWORKS FOR JOURNALISM

Broadly speaking, there are three dominant paradigms used to teach these ethics in journalism. Deontological ethics, based on the teachings of Immanuel Kant, is a "rule" based system of ethics. This approach has questionable utility for UK journalists, whose rules are set by various codes of practice which have repeatedly failed to ensure press standards. For example, the phone hacking scandal happened despite the existence of these codes.

Utilitarianism is also used to teach what's called "consequential ethics" – a system famously encapsulated by the maxim of finding "the greatest good for the greatest number." This is also problematic for journalists reporting issues that affect minorities or people outside the "imagined community" of their outlet's news audience.

The virtue ethics of Aristotle is the third dominant approach to teaching ethical philosophy. As with the pursuit of "objectivity" and "balance," this is about finding virtue through the "golden mean"—a "middle state" between two extremes. This can be interpreted as equal, or "balanced" reporting of the perspective of both the refugees and their persecutors.

OBJECTIVITY ISN'T ENOUGH

When media educators are asked about teaching ethics they rely on the mantra of "truth, accuracy and objectivity." This is despite research criticising the concept of objectivity as a "strategic ritual," a term coined by sociologist Gaye Tuchman to describe how journalists use objectivity to describe what they do and to protect themselves from professional criticism.

There are very few journalists who defend their trade on the basis that it is objective, truthful or accurate. Journalists and editors used the "fourth estate" defence throughout the Leveson enquiry. In a good example of this, the editor of the Daily Mail Paul Dacre argued, that journalists:

> ...passionately believe that their papers give voice to the voiceless and expose the misdeeds of the rich, the powerful and the pompous.

This is instructive because justice is the only defence of journalism worthy of consideration. Many years of being committed to "truth, accuracy and objectivity" has created a journalistic paradigm which has failed the very people it is supposed to serve: people fleeing persecution and poverty overseas and people living in poverty in the UK. The pursuit of justice should be placed at the heart of journalism education and practice.

1. When discussing matters of social justice, the author suggests that there are certain ethical considerations that must be kept in mind, such as the language journalists use to describe their subjects. What is some language you've seen in social justice stories that you think adds a form of bias to the story, either positive or negative? Do you think journalists should be careful with how they explain situations to prevent showing a bias against marginalized people in their stories?

2. Journalism is supposed to be impartial and objective, as the author notes. But many journalists also claim to be giving "voice to the voiceless" and "speaking truth to power." Do you think journalists covering social justice issues—such as the refugee crisis—should strive to be objective, or is it acceptable for them to use their platform to promote social justice? Does your opinion change if the journalists are writing about an issue you don't feel is as important? Explain your reasoning.

CHAPTER 6

WHAT ORDINARY CITIZENS SAY

Citizens have incredibly diverse views on matters of social justice. Some feel that you can never do enough to promote equality, while others discuss social justice issues as if they are problematic, and as if the people who believe in them are merely troublemakers. If you read the comments posted alongside online news articles about matters of social justice, you'll see readers arguing about the importance of the story, with some claiming more needs to be done and others calling out the journalists and their subjects as "social justice warriors" who seek to take away one group's freedom in order to give it to another class of people. As you'll learn in this chapter, everyone—from everyday citizens to well-known celebrities—has an opinion on matters of equality, and they express them in just as many different ways, from writing about their views to protesting publicly.

"DISABILITY, HUMAN RIGHTS AND JUSTICE," BY DEBORA DINIZ, LÍVIA BARBOSA, AND WEDERSON RUFINO DOS SANTOS, FROM *INTERNATIONAL JOURNAL ON HUMAN RIGHTS*, DECEMBER 2009

1 INTRODUCTION

To inhabit a body with physical, intellectual or sensory impairment is one of the many ways of existing in the world. Among the narratives of inequality that are expressed in the body, disability studies appeared as the late comers in the humanities and social sciences. Heirs to gender studies, feminists and anti-racists, the social model of disability proposed a redefinition of the meaning of living in a body that had been considered, for a long time, abnormal (DINIZ, 2007, p. 9). As for sexism or racism, this new expression of oppression led to the creation of a neologism: *disablism* (DINIZ, 2007, p. 9). Disablism is a result of the culture of normality, in which the impairments are the target of oppression and discrimination(inserir nota 2). Normality, which can either be understood as a biomedical expectation of standard functioning for the species or as a moral precept for productivity and adaptation to social norms, was challenged by the understanding that disability is not only a biomedical concept but a political one as well. Disability expresses the oppression of the body with impairments: the concept of a disabled body or person with disabilities should be understood in political terms and no longer strictly in biomedical terms.

This change of the body with impairments from a medical problem to disability as oppression is challenging for the establishment of public and social policies (DINIZ, 2007, p. 11) [...] Disability is not limited to a list of diseases and impairments that come from biomedical knowledge (DINIZ et al., 2009, p. 21). Disability is now considered to be the patterns of inequality that are imposed by environments with barriers on a body with impairments. Therefore, the United Nations Convention on the Rights of Persons with Disabilities refers to participation as a parameter for the formulation of policies aimed at this population, defining people with disabilities as "those who have physical, intellectual or sensory impairments, which, in interaction with various barriers, may hinder their full and effective participation in society with others" (UNITED NATIONS [UN], 2006a, Article 1). Disability is not only what medical discourse describes but specifically the restriction of participation caused by social barriers.

Brazil signed the Convention on the Rights of Persons with Disabilities in 2008. This means a new concept of disability must guide political actions to ensure justice for this population. According to the 2000 Census, 14.5% of Brazilians are living with disabilities (BRAZILIAN INSTITUTE OF GEOGRAPHY AND STATISTICS [IBGE], 2000). The criteria used by the 2000 Census to calculate the size of the population with disability were markedly biomedical, such as difficulty in seeing, hearing, or moving. This is due not only to the biomedical model currently in force in the planning and management of public policies for this population in Brazil but mainly due to the difficulty of measuring what is considered participation restriction by the interaction between the body and the social environment.

The Convention on the Rights of Persons with Disabilities does not ignore the body, as it states "impairments of a physical, intellectual or sensory nature" (UN, 2006a, Article 1.). It is the interaction between the impairments and the social barriers that restrict people's effective participation. According to the Convention, the new understanding of disability should not ignore the bodily impairments, nor is it restricted to listing them. This redefinition of disability as a combination of a biomedical framework, which lists bodily impairments, and a human rights perspective, which denounces this type of oppression, was not a creation of the United Nations alone. For over four decades, the so-called social model of disability provoked the international political and academic debate on the failure of the biomedical concept of disability to promote equality between disabled and non-disabled people (BARTON, 1998, p. 25; BARNES *et al*, 2002, p. 4).

The biomedical model of disability claims that there is a causal relationship between the impairments and the social disadvantages experienced by people with disabilities. This thesis was challenged by the social model, which not only challenged the medical power over bodily impairments but also showed how the body is not a destiny of exclusion (BARNES *et al*, 2002 p. 9; TREMAINE, 2002 p. 34). The social meaning attributed to these impairments is that they are a natural disadvantage, which historically meant that bodily impairments were seen as bad luck or personal tragedy (BARNES *et al*, 2002, p. 6). If in the 19th century the biomedical model was a kind of redemption from religious narratives, which described impairments as the result of sin or divine wrath, today it is the biomedical authority which is being challenged by the social model of disability (FOUCAULT, 2004, p. 18). The criticism of medicalization suggests the inadequacy of the biomedical discourse to evaluate the participation constraints imposed by social environments with barriers. Therefore, for the United Nations Convention on the Rights of Persons with Disabilities, the disadvantage is not inherent to the body, but the result of values, attitudes and practices that discriminate against disabled people (DINIZ *et al*, 2009, p. 21).

This paper demonstrates how disability studies reinforced the understanding of disability as a social disadvantage, challenging the biomedical narrative about what is normal and pathological. Through a historical review of the main ideas of the social model of disability, the article draws a picture of the concept of disability as a restriction on participation. This was the concept adopted by the United Nations Convention on the Rights of Persons with Disabilities, which was ratified by Brazil in 2008.

2 DISABILITIES AND IMPAIRMENTS

There are at least two ways of understanding disability. The first way understands it as an expression of human diversity. A body with impairments belongs to someone who experiences impairments of a physical, intellectual, or sensory nature. But the social barriers are the ones that, by ignoring the bodies with impairments, force the experience of inequality. Oppression is not an attribute of the impairment itself but the result of non-inclusive societies. The second way of understanding disability claims that it is a natural disadvantage, and efforts should be focused on repairing the impairments in order to ensure that all people can operate in a typical pattern for the species. In this interpretative process, bodily impairments are classified as undesirable and not simply as a neutral expression of human diversity, as one must understand racial, generational, or gender diversity. The body with impairments should undergo a metamorphosis to normality, be it through rehabilitation, genetics, or educational practices. These two narratives are not mutually exclusive, although they point to different perspectives regarding the challenge posed by disability and human rights.

For the social model of disability, ensuring equality between people with and without disability should not be reduced to the supply of goods and biomedical services: as with racial, generational or gender issues, disability is essentially a human rights issue (DINIZ, 2007, p. 79). Human rights have an important claim to universal validity, which is to return the responsibility for the inequalities to oppressive social constructions (SEN, 2004). This means that impairments acquire meaning only when converted into experiences through social interaction. Not everyone with impairments experiences discrimination, oppression, or inequality, because it is the relationship between the body and the society which produces disability (DINIZ, 2007, p. 23). The greater the social barriers, the greater the participation constraints imposed on disabled people.

For the biomedical model of disability, a body with impairments should be the object of biomedical knowledge intervention. Impairments are classified by medical narratives, which describe them as natural and undesirable disadvantages. Rehabilitation practices or healing are offered and even imposed on bodies in order to reverse or mitigate the signs of abnormality. The result is that the closer to the simulacra of normality, the greater the success of the medicalization of impairments (THOMAS, 2002, p. 41). Educational practices comprise another universe for the taming of bodies: the controversy over oralist or manualist practices for deaf children is an example of different perspectives regarding how the deaf shall dwell in non-bilingual societies (LANE, 1997, p. 154). This was actually a controversy covered by the Convention on the Rights of Persons with Disabilities, which recognizes the "facilitation of learning sign language and promotion of the linguistic identity of the deaf community" (UN, 2006a, article 24, 3b).

Disability has been understood as a personal or family destiny according to religious explanations, which was understood either as misfortune or as a blessing in almost all societies (LAKSHMI, 2008). The challenge of the mystical and religious narrative by the biomedical narrative was received as an important step towards ensuring equality (BARTON, 1998, p. 23; COURTINE, 2006, p. 305). The origins of the barriers were no longer sin, guilt, or bad luck but genetics, embryology, degenerative diseases, traffic accidents, or aging. The biomedical narrative marked the dichotomy between normal and pathological since the impairments are only defined when contrasted with an ideal of the body without them. The challenge now is to refute the description of a body with impairments as abnormal. Abnormality is an aesthetic judgment and, therefore, a moral value on life styles, not the result of a universal and absolute catalog about bodies (DINIZ, 2007, p. 23).

3 THE GENESIS OF THE SOCIAL MODEL

One of the early attempts to bring disability close to the culture of human rights was made in England in the 1970's (UNION OF THE PHYSICALLY IMPAIRED AGAINST SEGREGATION [UPIAS], 1976). The first generation of scholars defending the social model of disability was inspired by historical materialism and sought to explain oppression through the core values of capitalism, such as ideas of productive and functional bodies (DINIZ, 2007, p. 23). Bodies with impairments would be useless to the productive rationale in an economic structure that is not open to diversity. The biomedical model, on the other hand, indicated that the experience of segregation, unemployment, low education, among many other expressions of inequality, was caused by the inability of the body with impairments to do productive work. Today, the centrality of historical materialism is considered insufficient to explain the challenges imposed by disability in environments with barriers, but one must recognize the originality of this first movement to empower the social model of disability (CORKER, SHAKESPEARE, 2002, p. 3).

Other approaches emerged in disability studies, but the social model has remained hegemonic. The feminist and phenomenological approaches gained ground in the debate, expanding the narratives about the meanings of disability in cultures of normality (CORKER, SHAKESPEARE, 2002, p. 10). This was how impairments came to be described as neutral bodily attributes, and disability has summarized the oppression and discrimination suffered by people living with impairments in environments with barriers. By resisting the reduction of disability simply to impairments, the social model of disability offered new tools for social transformation and the guarantee of rights. It was not biology that oppressed but the culture of normality, which described some bodies as undesirable.

This change of interpretation on disability, shifting from the inequality of the body to social structures, had two implications. The first was to undermine the authority of the corrective resources that biomedicine commonly offered as the only alternative for the well-being of people with disabilities. Disabled people could not deny the benefits of biomedical goods and services, but they could challenge the supremacy that healing and rehabilitation had attained, implying the idea that the body with impairments is abnormal and pathological (CANGUILHEM, 1995, p. 56).

The second implication was that the social model opened analytical possibilities for a new description of the meaning of living in a body with impairments. The private experience of being in a body with impairments caused a limited scope of care in the household, often condemning those with greater dependence to abandonment and institutionalization. By exposing the oppression of social structures, the social model showed that impairments are one of many ways of experiencing the body.

The central thesis of the social model has enabled a shift of disability from private to public spaces. Disability is not only a matter of privacy and family care but a matter of justice (NUSSBAUM, 2007, p. 35). This symbolic passage from the *domestic* to the *public* shook several biomedical assumptions about disability. It has been stated, for example, that disability is not abnormal, not being limited to stigma or shame because of difference. The critique of the biomedical model does not mean ignoring how technology ensures people's well being (DINIZ, MEDEIROS, 2004a, 1155). People with bodily impairments experience pain, get sick, and some need permanent care (KITTAY, 1998, p. 9). However, goods and services are biomedical responses to health needs and are, therefore, universal demands. Unlike non-disabled people, impairments comprise lifestyles for those who experience them. Therefore, there are social model theorists that explore the idea of disability as an identity or community, like cultural identities (LANE, 1997, p. 160).

With the social model, disability came to be understood as an experience of inequality shared by people with different types of impairments: not the blind, deaf, or people in wheelchairs in their particularities, but disabled people, discriminated and oppressed by the culture of normality. Just as there are a variety of bodies, there are a variety of ways to inhabit a body with impairments. It was by bringing the studies of disability and cultural studies together that the concept of oppression won argumentative legitimacy: despite the ontological differences imposed by each impairment of physical, intellectual, or sensory nature, the experience of living in a body with impairment is discriminated against by the culture of normality. The dichotomy normal and pathological, represented by the opposition of the body with and without impairments, opened way for a new strategy for political intervention, as envisaged by the Convention on the Rights of Persons with Disabilities (UN, 2006a). In addition to other forms of discrimination, the concept of discrimination in the Convention includes the denial of reasonable accommodation, which demonstrates the recognition of barriers as a preventable cause of inequalities experienced by disabled people.

The social model originally claimed that a body with impairments would not be able to endure the capitalistic system (BARTON, OLIVER, 1997). The centrality of the social model as a critique against capitalism was substituted by cultural studies, which distanced disability even more from biomedical authority over the body. It is also the culture of normality which oppresses the body with impairment and not only the economy (DINIZ, 2007, p. 77). Social model theorists have offered evidence that to inhabit a body with impairments does not necessarily mean a sentence of segregation (YOUNG, 1990, p. 215). In the last two decades, the growth of population studies on aging strengthened the argumentative strategy of the social model of disability as a human rights issue: a body with impairments is a shared experience with aging (WENDELL, 2001, p. 21; DINIZ, MEDEIROS, 2004b, 110).

4 THE WORLD HEALTH ORGANIZATION AND THE SOCIAL MODEL OF DISABILITY

The World Health Organization (WHO) has two classification references for describing the health conditions of individuals: the International Statistical Classification of Diseases and Related Health Problems, which is the tenth revision of the International Classification of Diseases (ICD-10) and the International Classification of Functioning, Disability and Health (ICF). The ICF was approved in 2001 and anticipates the main political challenge of the definition of disability proposed by the Convention on the Rights of Persons with Disabilities: the document establishes criteria for measuring the barriers and restriction of social participation. Until the publication of the ICF, the WHO had adopted strictly biomedical language for the classification of bodily impairments, which is why the document is considered a milestone in the legitimization of the social model in the field of public health and human rights (DINIZ, 2007, p. 53).

The shift from the biomedical model to the social model of disability was the result of an extensive debate in the consultative stages of the ICF. The document that preceded it, the International Classification of Impairments, Disabilities, and Handicaps (ICIDH), assumed a causal link between impairments, disabilities, and handicaps (WHO, 1980). In this interpretative model of disability, a body with impairments would experience restrictions that led to social disadvantage. The disadvantage would be the result of impairments; therefore, the emphasis was on models of healing or rehabilitation. For nearly 30 years, the biomedical model of disability was sovereign in the actions of the WHO, which meant the hegemony of a language focused on the rehabilitation or cure of impairments in public policies in several countries. In Brazil, the biomedical model is used in population research, healthcare, and, in large part, education and health policies for people with disabilities (FARIAS; BUCHALLA, 2005, p. 192).

The vocabulary proposed by the ICIDH in 1980 was widely criticized by the emerging disability studies (WHO, 1980). There were different levels in the debate, but one was particularly embodied by the text of the Convention on the Rights of Persons with Disabilities: linguistic sensitivity towards the description of disability as a human rights issue, not just a biomedical one. As in studies of race and gender, biology and culture impose a permanent pendulum between what is defined as the fate of the body or the social oppression of the body. In feminist studies, the dichotomy between nature and culture was deconstructed in its own terms; the constitutive nature of sex to explain the existence of gender was ignored: sex and gender are interchangeable categories for the analysis of sexism (BUTLER, 2003, p. 25).

A similar analytic turn was triggered in disability studies to face *disablism*, the ideology that oppresses a body with impairments. The first generation of the social model sustained that the body should be ignored, as its emergence would facilitate the biomedical understanding of disability as a personal tragedy (DINIZ, 2007, p. 43). Adopting this posture, the study of aspects of the body with impairments, such as pain, addiction, dependency, or weaknesses would be to surrender to the concept of biomedical control of disability as a deviation or abnormality (WENDELL, 1996, p. 117, MORRIS, 2001, p. 9). The result was the silencing of the body as an instance of habitability, and as a locus in which to describe disabilities. The semblance of normality for all bodies set the tone of the debates and political struggles of the 1970s for the social model.

But the silence was challenged by the emergence of other perspectives into the social model, especially feminism. Not coincidentally, the social model of disability began with white adult men in wheelchairs (DINIZ, 2007, p. 60), a group of people for whom social barriers would be essentially physical. The inclusion of this group would not subvert the social order, as in their specific case the simulacrum of normality was effective to demonstrate the success of inclusion. Even today road signs and public representations of disability indicate someone in a wheelchair as the icon. The metonymy of disability by the wheelchair should not be underestimated in a culture of normality filled with barriers to social participation for people with other impairments, for whom these barriers are not only physical.

The first feminists working in the social model launched the issue of intellectual impairments and care to the center of the discussions (KITTAY, 1998, p. 29). To seriously consider the diversity of impairments was not resolved with the simulacrum of normality; it was necessary to challenge the culture of normality. Social barriers for the inclusion of a person with severe intellectual impairments are multiple, difficult to measure, and permeate all spheres of public life. This is how the narratives about the body with impairments and the theme of care as a human need came to be discussed in disability studies. However, to consider care as a human need is also to bring the issue of disability closer to gender and family studies. The issue of gender equality serves as a background for the Convention on the Rights of Persons with Disabilities, from the preamble to the specific sections on the protection of girls and women with disabilities, and the role of families of people with disabilities (UN, 2006a).

The ICF, thus, was born after a long process of reflection on the potential and limits of biomedical and social models of disability. In a position of dialogue between the two models, the proposal of the document is to launch a bio-psychosocial vocabulary to describe disability. Despite the diversity of experiences of people with impairments related both to the body and to society, the ICF has universal ambitions (THE WORLD HEALTH ORGANIZATIONS' COLLABORATING CENTER FOR THE FAMILY OF INTERNATIONAL CLASSIFICATIONS, 2003, p. 18). This universal claim can be understood in two ways. First as recognition of the political force of the social model of disability for the revision of the document: from a classification of abnormal bodies (ICIDH) to a complex evaluation of the relationship between the individual and society (CIF). A disabled person is not simply a body with impairments but a person with impairments living in an environment with barriers. The second way of understanding the universal ambition of the ICF is also a result of the social model: the body with impairments is not a personal tragedy, but a life condition for those who experience the benefits of biotechnology and aging. Old age and disability are concepts brought closer together by the CIF and the new generation of disability theorists (DINIZ, 2007, p. 70).

But while progressing from the ICIDH towards the ICF, one of the most sensitive issues was how to describe disability. The same challenge was present in the elaboration of the Convention on the Rights of Persons with Disabilities. The ICIDH used the concepts of impairments, disabilities, and handicaps. The demand from the social model of disability was to describe impairments as a neutral expression of the diversity of the human body, understanding the body as an instance of individual habitability – therefore, diverse in its condition. The vocabulary proposed by the ICIDH classified physical diversity as a result of diseases or abnormalities, besides considering that the disadvantages were caused by the inability of the impaired body to adapt to social life.

The revision of the ICF tried to resolve this controversy by incorporating the main criticisms of the social model (THE WORLD HEALTH ORGANIZATIONS' COLLABORATING CENTER FOR THE FAMILY OF INTERNATIONAL CLASSIFICATIONS, 2003, p. 32). According to this new vocabulary, disability is an umbrella term that embraces the body with impairments, activity limitations, or participation restrictions. This means that disability is not limited to impairments; it is the negative outcome of the insertion of a body with impairments into social environments that are insensitive to people's physical diversity. There is no primordial meaning in the body, so any attempt to reduce it to a certain fate must be ignored. This redefinition conformed to the critique proposed by the social model: disability is a cultural experience and not just the result of a biomedical diagnosis of abnormalities. It was also this spirit that has abandoned the notion of "handicap", especially because of its etymology which referred to disabled people as beggars ("cap in hand") (DINIZ, 2007, p. 35).

The Convention on the Rights of Persons with Disabilities has proposed a concept of disability that recognizes the experience of oppression suffered by disabled people. The new approach overcomes the idea of impairment as synonymous for people with disabilities, recognizing the restriction of participation as being the main aspect that causes the disability to be perceived as inequality. The importance of the Convention is to constitute a document of reference for the protection of the rights of disabled people in countries around the world. In all the signatory countries, the Convention is taken as the basis for the construction of social policies regarding the identification of both the subject of social protection as well as the rights to be guaranteed. The ICF, in turn, provides objective tools for the identification of the different expressions of *disablism*, enabling better targeting of policies.

5 FINAL CONSIDERATIONS

The recognition of the body with impairments as an expression of human diversity is recent and still a challenge for democratic societies and public policies. The history of the medicalization and normalization of disabled bodies by biomedical and religious knowledge superimposed a history of segregating people in long-term institutions. Only recently were the demands of these people recognized as a human rights issue. The United Nations Convention on the Rights of Persons with Disabilities established a new framework for understanding disability (UN, 2006a). Ensuring decent life no longer limits itself solely to the provision of goods and health care services, but also requires the removal of barriers and the guarantee of a social environment that is accessible to all people with physical, intellectual, or sensory impairments.

The social disadvantage experienced by disabled people is not a sentence of nature but the result of disablism, which describes bodily impairments as abject to social life. The social model of disability challenged the narratives of misfortune and personal tragedy that confined disabled people to the domestic space of secrecy and guilt. The social model not only proposed a new concept of disability in dialogue with theories of inequality and oppression, but also revolutionized the way of identifying the body and how it relates to societies. The International Classification of Functioning, Disability and Health (ICF) of the World Health Organization has proposed a vocabulary for the identification of persons with disabilities in order to guide public policies in each country. Since 2007, the

ICF has been adopted in the Brazilian legislation for the implementation of the Continuous Cash Transfer Program (CCT), a welfare income transfer to the disabled and poor elderly. The trend is that the ICF is being used in the identification of disability for social welfare policy as well as in all other Brazilian public policies.

The adoption of the Convention on the Rights of Persons with Disabilities recognizes the issue of disability as a question of justice, human rights, and promoting equality. The Convention was ratified in 2008, which will require the revision of infra-constitutional laws and establishing new bases for the formulation of public policies for the disabled population. One of the requirements of the Convention is the immediate review of all laws and state actions related to the population with disabilities. Compliance with this measure will bring direct results to guarantee the well being and promotion of dignity for people with disabilities in Brazil.

1. The authors discuss the oppression that people with disabilities face. After reading the article, as well as others in this book, do you believe that disabled or differently abled citizens need to fight for equality and social justice as much as other marginalized communities? Explain.

2. As with other marginalized classes, language is important, and the authors discuss how the word "handicapped" is not appropriate to use when discussing differently abled people. Do you think that the language we use impacts how we view the need for social justice? Do you think referring to these people as "disabled" or "handicapped" allows people to think of them as not equal? What language would you use instead?

"SEATTLE TEACHERS' STRIKE A WIN FOR SOCIAL JUSTICE," BY JEFF BRYANT, FROM *PEOPLE'S ACTION BLOG*, SEPTEMBER 19, 2015

Teachers unions are routinely vilified by pundits and politicians on the right and left these days. So when schoolteachers in Seattle began the school year by going on strike, the editorial board of The Seattle Times was quick to accuse the teachers of "demanding too much."

The editors called the strike "illegal," "disruptive," and "a symbol of excess for those who oppose more school spending."

What seemed to bother this august body most was that teachers' demands would "have a negative effect on broader efforts to reform the state education system."

Now that a tentative settlement is in place (to be approved by the teachers on Sunday), and it appears teachers have been victorious in getting most of their demands met, it's apparent what teachers were fighting for were issues that are in the best interests of their students.

"It's a win for public education in many ways," says Jesse Hagopian, a prominent spokesperson for the striking teachers. In a phone conversation, Hagopian—a Garfield High School teacher, editor of the book "More Than a Score: The New Uprising Against High-Stakes Testing," and recipient of the 2013 "Secondary School Teacher of Year" award—tells me in a phone conversation, "For the first time, our union was able to make social justice the center of the debate. We took a huge step forward."

For sure, the Seattle teachers were demanding an increase in their pay. After all, as the local Fox News affiliate reports, teachers in one of America's most expensive cities to live in have gone six years without a cost-of-living increase and have received, over that time, a mere 8 percent increase in base salary from the district.

However, the pay increase—a bargaining position the teachers ultimately greatly compromised on—was just one item in a much more extensive list of demands that demonstrate how badly fans of education "reform" misrepresent and misunderstand what teachers unions often fight for.

STUDENT-CENTERED DEMANDS

Also in the settlement terms, according to a local television news outlet, were student-centered demands including requests for guaranteed 30 minutes of recess for all elementary students, additional staff such as school counselors and therapists, a reduction in the over-testing of students, and the creation of new teams in 30 schools to ensure equitable learning opportunities and treatment of students regardless of race.

While recess may seem to be an unworthy demand to the reform-minded editors of the Times, classroom teachers understand it to be something critical to the health, development, and academic success of their students, as numerous research reports have found.

Having access to school counselors, therapists, and other specialists is critical to many students, but in inadequately funded school districts, such as Seattle, these are the positions that are routinely the first to be cut.

The demand for less testing is also, ultimately, a student-centered demand. As Hagopian explains, this time to Erin Middlewood for The Progressive magazine, "'We oppose these tests because there are too many of them and they're narrowing the curriculum and they're making our kids feel bad, but they're also part of maintaining institutional racism,' says Hagopian, who serves as an adviser to Garfield's Black Student Union."

Hagopian sees the increasingly popular campaign to opt out of standardized tests as being connected to the Black Lives Matter movement because money that should be used to support and educate children and youth of color is being directed to punitive measures such as testing and incarceration.

The connection of education injustice, represented by standardized testing, to broader social injustices is also driving teachers' demands for equity teams in schools to address widespread imbalances in disciplinary action based on race. Numerous studies have shown black students—especially in Seattle—are far more apt to face harsh disciplinary measures including suspensions and expulsions, and Seattle teachers are wise to insist the district address this disparity.

SOCIAL JUSTICE FOR TEACHERS, TOO

For sure, student-centered demands coming from the teachers are related to teachers' work issues too.

In their demands for less testing, teachers also asked for, and received, relief from having those test results used in their performance evaluations. Although test-based evaluations have been a favorite policy point for the Obama administration and other reform advocates, leading experts have deemed this approach unreliable and invalid as the formulas used in this process can lead to results that can vary dramatically from year to year for each individual teacher.

The district's demand for an extended school day, an issue teachers objected to at first but now seem to be accepting, is another instance where teachers' working conditions are intertwined with student learning. What's ironic about extended-day mandates—another favorite policy point from the reform community—is that the demands usually come from those who are most critical of local public schools. If these critics believe schools are doing such a bad job, why would they insist students spend more time in them?

Further, those who demand students spend more time in school don't generally consider what exactly that extra time—in this case, 20 minutes—is supposed to be used for. Adding an extra five minutes to core subject classes makes little sense. Adding extra time for, say, tutoring sessions or study time also hardly seems impactful, and may necessitate more costs.

What's most likely to happen, Hagopian laments in his phone conversation with me, is that teachers will ultimately see the extra time taken out of their time to plan their lessons, examine student work, and collaborate with their peers—all of which are teacher activities that have enormous effects on student learning.

PARENTS CAN RELATE

Rather than angering Seattle parents, the striking teachers drew their support. As a Huffington Post reporter observes, "More than 4,000 people have signed a Change.org petition calling on parents to support the union. Several parents have co-authored op-eds advocating for the teachers' demands."

The local NBC News affiliate reports parents rallied in front of the school district's administrative center in support of the teachers. "I think the district needs to buck up," a parent is quoted. "I don't want the teachers to fold."

In response to The Seattle Times' indignation with the teachers, blog posts and a Facebook page went up urging people to cancel their subscriptions to the paper.

Joining in the support of the teachers was the Seattle city council that voted unanimously to support the teachers and directed the city's community centers to care for elementary-age students at no additional costs to parents.

"The biggest win for us [teachers] is not what's in the contract," Hagopian explains to me, "but in the solidarity of the community – the support we received from parents, the local chapter of the NAACP, the council, everyone."

Hagopian points to a "Soup for Teachers" Facebook page that was used to organize thousand of parents to bring food to teachers on the picket lines, and he notes even as news of the settlement was breaking, supporters were rallying to their cause. The outpouring of support prompts Hagopian to regret somewhat the compromise on pay the teachers took. He calls the 2 percent increase above base pay for the least paid teachers in the district a "punch in the gut."

Despite Hagopian's regret on teacher pay, Seattle teachers got most of what they wanted because their demands were undoubtedly in the best interests of the students.

CONNECTING THE DOTS

Writing for the feminist news outlet Dame Magazine, Sarah Jaffe sources the success of the Seattle teachers to the tactics used in the Chicago teachers' strike of 2012.

"Chicago's teachers were legally prevented from striking over anything but wages and benefits," she writes, "but their organizing, their speeches, their actions highlighted everything from the lack of air-conditioning in the schools to the forcing of students to cross gang lines when their neighborhood school was shut down. Their working conditions, they noted, were their students' learning conditions. In Seattle, the teachers have been able to explicitly make issues like recess or racist suspension policies part of the bargaining process."

"We've been connecting the dots," Hagopian says.

1. Labor unions are viewed as both incredibly helpful to workers and as taking advantage of employers, depending on whom you ask. In this article, it is suggested that the teachers' union got what they wanted—including a living wage—because the majority of their demands were made to improve the lives of the students, and not the teachers themselves. When it comes to matters of social justice, do you think that resolutions that can help more than the vulnerable group are more likely to lead to that group getting the solution they're seeking? Can you name other instances of this from history or the news?

2. The teachers in Seattle were supported by the parents of the students they taught, which likely helped their case. When it comes to issues of social injustice involving more marginalized groups—like Muslims or African Americans, or even women—do you think it's important that other groups— such as whites and men—support the issues? Do you think change can occur if these marginalized groups don't have support from other groups?

"COLIN KAEPERNICK PLEDGES $1 MILLION TO SOCIAL JUSTICE GROUPS AS MORE PLAYERS SIT," BY NADIA PRUPIS, FROM *COMMON DREAMS*, SEPTEMBER 2, 2016

"I'VE BEEN VERY BLESSED TO BE IN THIS POSITION AND MAKE THE KIND OF MONEY I DO, AND I HAVE TO HELP THESE PEOPLE. I HAVE TO HELP THESE COMMUNITIES"

San Francisco 49ers quarterback Colin Kaepernick's protest is growing, and with it, his mission.

When Kaepernick kneeled during the national anthem ahead of the 49ers' Thursday night preseason finale against the San Diego Chargers, he was joined by his teammate Eric Reid—while further up the coast, Seattle Seahawks cornerback Jeremy Lane also sat down in solidarity as the anthem played ahead of a game against the Oakland Raiders.

"I believe in what [Kaepernick] is doing," Reid told ESPN. "I believe that there are issues in this country—many issues, too many to name. It's not one particular issue. But there are people out there that feel there are injustices being made and happening in our country on a daily basis. I just wanted to show him I support him. I know there are other people in this country that feel the same way."

When the song ended, the two players stood and embraced. "It was amazing," Kaepernick told ESPN. "Me and Eric had many conversations and he approached me and said 'I support what you're doing, I support what your message is, let's think about how we can do this together.' We talked about it at length and we wanted to make sure the message that we're trying to send isn't lost with the actions that come along with it."

Those actions have now expanded, as Kaepernick on Thursday pledged to donate $1 million of his salary to community organizations focused on social justice causes.

"I've been very blessed to be in this position and make the kind of money I do, and I have to help these people. I have to help these communities," he said. "It's not right that they're not put in the position to succeed, or given the opportunities to succeed."

"The message is that we have a lot of issues in this country that we have to deal with. We have a lot of people that are oppressed, we have a lot of people that aren't treated equally, aren't given equal opportunities. Police brutality is a huge thing that needs to be addressed," he added.

In Oakland, Lane was the only member of either team to sit down during the anthem. He said he didn't know Kaepernick personally, but was "standing behind" him. After the game, he said, "It's something I plan to keep doing until I feel like justice is being served."

1. Football player Kaepernick chose to kneel during the national anthem as a form of protest against the social injustice faced by black Americans. Do you think Kaepernick's protest helped or hurt the fight for justice? Explain.

2. Kaepernick notes that he is in a position of privilege because of his high income and celebrity status, so he doesn't necessarily face the same issues that the average black man might confront. Do you think celebrities should use their platform to stand up for less privileged communities? Do you think that celebrity support helps promote social justice, or does it hurt it because they speak from a place of privilege?

"DON'T PLAY INTO TRUMP'S HANDS ON THE MUSLIM BAN," BY DINA EL-RIFAI, FROM *OTHERWORDS*, FEBRUARY 1, 2017

PLEASE DON'T REINFORCE IDEAS THAT PAINT US AS VIOLENT

I'm a Muslim woman and a social justice advocate.

I'm terrified, heartbroken, and outraged by Donald Trump's "Muslim ban." As I watched administrative chaos and rapidly organized protests unfold at airports all over America, I was overwhelmed with messages from friends fearing they'd never be able to see their loved ones again.

Though the executive order doesn't use these exact words, this is no doubt a Muslim ban.

It's not just that the countries Trump wants to prohibit immigration from—Libya, Yemen, Iraq, Iran, Syria, Sudan, and Somalia—are majority-Muslim. It's that religious minorities (i.e. anyone who isn't Muslim) from those countries will be prioritized for entry into the U.S.

Refugees, immigrants, and Muslims are human beings —regardless of their age, status, skills, or nation of origin. Many Americans realize this, which is why thousands have turned up at protests to speak out against the ban.

But while they mean well, non-Muslim opponents of the ban still have to be careful not to repeat dangerous stereotypes when pushing back against this extreme action.

For instance, you may have heard that Trump's order left off the Muslim-majority countries where President Trump has business deals—some of which, like Saudi Arabia and Egypt, happen to be where individuals who've carried out violent attacks hailed from.

All of that's true, of course, and there's value in pointing out Trump's unprecedented conflicts of interest.

But in reality, Muslims in these countries are the primary victims of extremist violence there. And suggesting that Trump should ban those countries too only encourages broadening the Muslim ban, not ending it.

Another common argument I've heard is that Muslim refugees and immigrants strengthen national security by acting as police informants and joining the military, and that this ban could break the bonds of trust that enable those partnerships.

It's true that Muslims are leading providers of tips to law enforcement agencies investigating "terrorism." But it's not like all Muslims are somehow connected to or aware of extremist plots. We're ordinary people, and we shouldn't have to be "useful" to law enforcement to deserve fundamental rights.

The narrative link between Islam and violence is

used to justify military intervention abroad, which in turn is used to justify suspicion of Muslims at home. Muslims are seen as potential "terrorists," to the point that the word is popularly linked with Islam—despite repeated horrific acts committed by white men in the U.S. in the name of Christianity or white nationalism.

This stereotyping feeds into increased hate crimes and harassment, as well as profiling and government surveillance of Muslims.

Sadly, Donald Trump isn't the first president to make things worse for Muslims.

The Obama administration's wars were often justified through the demonization and dehumanization of Muslims. So were its expansion of the drone program, unwarranted surveillance, militarization of our borders and policing, and record-breaking numbers of deportations.

Trump's latest action is reminiscent of past immigration bans, and the implications of where we could go from here are terrifying. Scary precedents include the ban on immigration from Asia and the great national shame of Japanese internment.

Only by acknowledging the history of these systems and policies—systems that existed long before Trump took office—can we understand how to resist them today.

Trump's Muslim ban has already been widely applied, and we can't ignore the threat of it growing. I, and so many Muslims, recognize this undeniable possibility. We're not safe. We're targets here and abroad.

So I'd ask this of my friends and neighbors: Don't

reinforce ideas that paint us as inherently violent and undermine our humanity. Reach out to us, support us, uplift our voices and humanity.

1. El-Rifai notes that the immigration ban signed by President Trump not only blocks immigrants from Muslim-majority countries, but also that immigrants from those countries who are not Muslim will be prioritized once immigration is allowed again. While some believe that this move is warranted because of terrorism, others suggest it is a move similar to when the Japanese citizens of America were put in internment camps during World War II. Do you think this kind of inequality is permissible during times of war and terror? Explain.

CONCLUSION

As you've now seen, social justice is not merely one issue, but is a collection of extremely difficult and complex matters that experts and everyday citizens have a hard time agreeing on. But most people will agree that social justice matters—or at least, their version of it matters.

Governments and politicians, as well as advocacy organizations, work tirelessly to figure out what "social justice" means, and what they can do to reach a point where they believe justice will have been achieved. For some, that means making sure everyone has equal opportunities, equal access to wealth, and equal rights. For others, it means making sure people are treated equally but that no one is given a handout or any help that someone else isn't getting. For still others, it means that their own rights are the priority and that no one else can do anything to affect the access and opportunities they have. There isn't necessarily a right approach to social justice—which is why it's such a complicated issue.

But as the articles in this book have demonstrated, it's possible to hold multiple views about an issue, and to find many different ways in which to promote equality for all without having to give up any of your own rights or privileges. Colin Kaepernick demonstrates that he could fight for the rights of African Americans even though he has a level of privilege that most African Americans do not currently experience, while authors like Jemina Napier, Jessica Tyrrell, and Timothy Frayling show that people from a typically non-marginalized class can still be vulnerable, and that people can experience life as part of many different marginalized groups.

What all of the authors have expressed, however, is that there is a chance for change, and that no matter which vulnerable group a person belongs to, there is someone out there fighting for justice for them, regardless of their race, sex, class, gender, or religion. And that's the biggest lesson of social justice: everyone deserves it, and there will always be someone fighting for it.

BIBLIOGRAPHY

Bryant, Jeff. "Seattle Teachers' Strike A Win For Social Justice." *People's Action Blog*, September 19, 2015. http://www.commondreams.org/views/2015/09/19/seattle-teachers-strike-win-social-justice.

Clinton, Hillary Rodham. "Women's Rights Are Human Rights." The United Nations Fourth World Conference on Women, Plenary Session in Beijing, China, September 5, 2015. http://gos.sbc.edu/c/clinton.html.

Diniz, Debora, Livia Barbosa and Wederson Rufino dos Santos. "Disability, Human Rights and Justice." *International Journal on Human Rights*, December 2009. http://www.scielo.br/pdf/sur/v6n11/en_04.pdf.

Dorn, James A. "Inequality: The Rhetoric and Reality." *Foundation for Economic Education*, June 22, 2015. https://fee.org/articles/inequality-the-rhetoric-and-reality.

Edelman, Marian Wright. "Urban Food Deserts Threaten Children's Health." *OtherWords*, January 11, 2010. https://otherwords.org/urban_food_deserts_threaten_childrens_health.

El-Rifai, Dina. "Don't Play Into Trump's Hands on the Muslim Ban." *OtherWords*, February 1, 2017. http://otherwords.org/dont-play-into-trumps-hands-on-the-muslim-ban.

Frayling, Timothy and Jessica Tyrrell. "Why Life is Tougher for Short Men and Overweight Women." *The Conversation*, March 9, 2016. https://theconversation.com/why-life-is-tougher-for-short-men-and-overweight-women-54671.

Fulton, Deirdre. "Tensions High as Combat-Ready Police Confront National Black Lives Matter Protests." *Common Dreams*, July 11, 2016. http://www.commondreams.org/news/2016/07/11/tensions-high-combat-ready-police-confront-national-black-lives-matter-protests.

Gardner, Cooper. "Phoenix Residents, Mayor and Police Vow to Build Solutions in Black Lives Matter Meeting." *Cronkite News*, July 20, 2016. https://cronkitenews.azpbs.org/2016/07/20/vow-to-build-solutions-black-lives-matter-meeting.

Greco, Emily Schwartz. "Byline Inequality Matters." *OtherWords*, August 19, 2015. https://otherwords.org/byline-inequality-matters.

Green, Kathryn. "Bring Social Justice in From the Cold as We Get Closer to a Global Climate Change Deal." *The Conversation*, September 24, 2014. https://theconversation.com/bring-social-justice-in-from-the-cold-as-we-get-closer-to-a-global-climate

-change-deal-32120.
Gurciullo, Brianna, Karen Mawdsley and Katie Campbell. "Pro-Legalization Groups Prepare for Marijuana Measures in 2016." *News 21*, August 15, 2015. http://weedrush.news21.com/pro-legalization-groups-prepare-for-marijuana-measures-in-2016.

Harkins, Steven. "Justice Should Be the Driving Force for Reporting on the Refugee Crisis." *The Conversation*, September 18, 2015. https://theconversation.com/justice-should-be-the-driving-force-for-reporting-on-the-refugee-crisis-47387.

Janoff-Bulman, Ronnie and Nate C. Carnes. "Social Justice and Social Order: Binding Moralities across the Political Spectrum." *PLOS One*, March 31, 2016. http://journals.plos.org/plosone/article?id=10.1371/journal.pone.0152479#sec020.

Kennedy, Sheila. "Report: Privatization Drives Inequality." *Inequality.org*, October 4, 2016. http://inequality.org/report-privatization-drives-inequality.

Knight, Nika. "Arizona Bill Would Ban Discussion of Social Justice, Solidarity in Schools." *Common Dreams*, January 13, 2017. http://www.commondreams.org/news/2017/01/13/arizona-bill-would-ban-discussion-social-justice-solidarity-schools.

Markham, Claire. "Paul Ryan Says the Catholic Charity Model Is the Solution to Poverty. Catholics Disagree." *Common Dreams*, September 2, 2016. http://www.commondreams.org/views/2016/09/02/paul-ryan-says-catholic-charity-model-solution-poverty-catholics-disagree.

Matthee, Keith. "Justifying the Use of Violence to Fight Social Injustice is a Recipe For Disaster." *The Conversation*, October 19, 2016. https://theconversation.com/justifying-the-use-of-violence-to-fight-social-injustice-is-a-recipe-for-disaster-66518.

Mezzadri, Alessandra. "Why Inequality Matters – For the Rich and the Poor." *The Conversation*, October 2, 2015. https://theconversation.com/why-inequality-matters-for-the-rich-and-the-poor-47804.

Morial, Marc. "We Still Need Black History Month." *OtherWords*, February 3, 2016. https://otherwords.org/we-still-need-black-history-month.

Napier, Jemina. "Deaf or Blind People Can't Serve on juries – Here's Why Law Needs to Change." *The Conversation*, October 24, 2016. https://theconversation.com/deaf-or-blind-people-cant-serve-on-juries-heres-why-law-needs-to-change-67418.

Napier, Jemina. "When Dealing with the Police, Deaf People Are at a Major Disadvantage." *The Conversation*, August 3, 2016. https://theconversation.com/when-dealing-with-the-police-deaf-people-are-at-a-major-disadvantage-62027.

Prupis, Nadia. "Colin Kaepernick Pledges $1 Million to Social Justice Groups as More Players Sit." *Common Dreams*, September 2, 2016. http://www.commondreams.org/news/2016/09/02/colin-kaepernick-pledges-1-million-social-justice-groups-more-players-sit.

Revkin, Andrew. "Will Trump's Climate Team Accept Any 'Social Cost of Carbon'?" *ProPublica*, January 11, 2017. https://www.propublica.org/article/will-trumps-climate-team-accept-any-social-cost-of-carbon.

Sexton, Joe. "Alleged Chicago Assault Reignites Issue of Hate Crimes Against Whites." *ProPublica*, January 5, 2017. https://www.propublica.org/article/alleged-chicago-assault-reignites-issue-of-hate-crimes-against-whites.

United States Supreme Court. *Boy Scouts of America et al. v. Dale* (530 U.S. 640). June 28, 2000. https://supreme.justia.com/cases/federal/us/530/640/case.html.

United States Supreme Court. *Pena-Rodriguez v. Colorado* (580 U.S. ___). March 6, 2017. https://supreme.justia.com/cases/federal/us/580/15-606.

United States Supreme Court. *Plessy v. Ferguson* (163 U.S. 537). May 18, 1896. https://supreme.justia.com/cases/federal/us/163/537/case.html.

United States Supreme Court. *United States v. Virginia et al.* (518 U.S. 515). June 26, 1996. https://supreme.justia.com/cases/federal/us/518/515/case.html.

CHAPTER NOTES

CHAPTER 1: WHAT THE EXPERTS SAY

EXCERPT FROM "SOCIAL JUSTICE AND SOCIAL ORDER: BINDING MORALITIES ACROSS THE POLITICAL SPECTRUM" BY RONNIE JANOFF-BULMAN AND NATE C. CARNES

1. Janoff-Bulman R, Sheikh S, Hepp S. Proscriptive versus prescriptive morality: Two faces of moral regulation. Journal of Personality and Social Psychology. 2009;96: 521–537. doi: 10.1037/a0013779. pmid:19254101.

2. Janoff-Bulman R, Carnes NC. Surveying the moral landscape: Moral motives and group-based moralities. Personality and Social Psychology Review. 2013;17: 219–236. doi: 10.1177/1088868313480274. pmid:23504824.

3. Janoff-Bulman R, Carnes NC. Moral context matters: A reply to Graham. Personality and Social Psychology Review. 2013;17: 242–247. doi: 10.1177/1088868313492021. pmid:23861353.

4. Hofmann W, Wisneski DC, Brandt MJ, Skitka, LJ. Morality in everyday life. Science. 2014;345: 1340–1343. doi: 10.1126/science.1251560. pmid:25214626.

5. Gray K, Young L, Waytz A. Mind perception is the essence of morality. Psychological Inquiry. 2012;23: 101–124 pmid:22754268.

6. Tomasello M, Vaish A. Origins of human cooperation and morality. Annual Review of Psychology. 2013;64: 231–55. doi: 10.1146/annurev-psych-113011-143812. pmid:22804772.

7. Janoff-Bulman R. To provide or protect: Motivational bases of political liberalism and conservatism. Psychological Inquiry. 2009;20: 120–128.

8. Graham J, Nosek BA, Haidt J, Iyer R, Koleva S, Ditto PH. Mapping the moral domain. Journal of Personality and Social Psychology, 2011;101: 366–385. doi: 10.1037/a0021847. pmid:21244182.

9. Haidt J. The new synthesis in moral psychology. Science. 2007;316: 998–1002. pmid:17510357.

10. Haidt J, Joseph C. Intuitive ethics: How innately prepared intuitions generate culturally variable virtues. Daedalus. 2004;Fall: 55–66.

11. Haidt J, Joseph C. The moral mind: How 5 sets of innate moral intuitions guide the development of many culture-specific virtues, and perhaps even modules. In: Carruthers P, Laurence S, Stich S, editors. The Innate Mind, Vol. 3. New York: Oxford; 2007. pp. 367–392.

12. Graham J, Haidt J, Nosek, B. Liberals and conservatives use different sets of moral foundations. Journal of Personality and Social Psychology. 2009;96: 1029–1046. doi: 10.1037/a0015141. pmid:19379034.

13. Haidt J. The righteous mind: Why good people are divided by politics and religion. New York: Pantheon Books; 2012.

14. Haidt J, Graham J. When morality opposes justice: Conservatives have moral intuitions that liberals may not recognize. Social Justice Research. 2007;20: 98–116.

15. Brickman P, Folger R, Goode E, Schul Y. Microjustice and macrojustice. In: Lerner MJ, Lerner SC, editors. The justice motive in social behavior. New York: Plenum; 1981. pp. 173–202.

16. Cohen RL. Distributive justice: Theory and research. Social Justice Research. 1987;1: 19–40.

17. Wenzel M. A social categorisation approach to distributive justice. European Review of Social Psychology. 2004;15: 219–257.

18. Graham J. Mapping the moral maps from alternate taxonomies to competing predictions. Personality and Social Psychology Review. 2013;17: 237–241. doi: 10.1177/1088868313492020. pmid:23861352.

19. Carnes NC, Janoff-Bulman R. Harm, Help, and the nature of (im)moral (in)action. Psychological Inquiry. 2012;23: 137–142.

20. Amodio DM, Jost JT, Master SL, Yee CM. Neurocognitive correlates of liberalism and conservatism. Nature neuroscience. 2007;10: 1246–1247 pmid:17828253.

21. Block J, Block JH. Nursery school personality and political orientation two decades later. Journal of Research in Personality. 2006;40: 734–749.

22. Fraley RC, Griffin BN, Belsky J, Roisman GI. Developmental antecedents of political ideology: A longitudinal investigation from birth to age 18. Psychological Science. 2012;23: 1425–1431. doi: 10.1177/0956797612440102. pmid:23054474.

23. Hibbing JR, Smith KB, Alford JR. Differences in negativity bias underlie variations in political ideology. Behavioral and Brain Sciences. 2014;37: 297–307. doi: 10.1017/S0140525X13001192. pmid:24970428

24. Inbar Y, Pizarro DA, Bloom P. Conservatives are more easily disgusted than liberals. Cognition and Emotion. 2009;4: 714–725.

25. Inbar Y, Pizarro DA, Iyer R, Haidt J. Disgust sensitivity, political conservatism, and voting. Social Psychological and Personality Science. 2012;3: 537–544.

26. Janoff-Bulman R, Carnes NC, & Sheikh S. Parenting and politics: Exploring early moral bases of political orientation. Journal of Social and Political Psychology. 2014;2: 43–60.

27. Jost JT, Glaser J, Kruglanski AW, Sulloway FJ. Political conservatism as motivated social cognition. Psychological Bulletin. 2003;129: 339–375. pmid:12784934.

28. Kanai R, Feilden T, Firth C, Rees G. Political orientations are correlated with brain structure in young adults. Current biology. 2011;21: 677–680. doi: 10.1016/j.cub.2011.03.017. pmid:21474316.

29. Lavine H, Burgess D, Snyder M, Transue J, Sullivan JL, Haney B, et al. Threat, authoritarianism and voting: An investigation of personality and persuasion. Personality and Social Psychology Bulletin. 1999; 25: 337–347.

30. McAdams DP, Albaugh M, Farber E, Daniels J, Logan R, Olson B. Family metaphors and moral intuitions: how conservatives and liberals narrate their lives. Journal of Personality and Social Psychology. 2008;95: 978–990. doi: 10.1037/a0012650. pmid:18808272.

31. McCrae RR. Social consequences of experiential openness. Psychological Bulletin. 1996; 120: 323–337. pmid:8900080.

32. Oxley DR, Smith KB, Alford JR, Hibbing MV, Miller JL, Scalero M, et al. Political attitudes vary with physiological traits. Science. 2008;321: 1667–1670. doi: 10.1126/science.1157627. pmid:18801995.

33. Rock M, Janoff-Bulman R. Where do we draw our lines? Politics, rigidity, and the role of self-regulation. Social Psychological and Personality Science. 2010;1: 26–33.

34. Shook N, Fazio RH. Political ideology, exploration of novel stimuli, and attitude formation. Journal of Experimental Social Psychology. 2009;45: 995–998.

35. Sheikh S, Janoff-Bulman R. Paradoxical consequences of prohibitions. Journal of Personality and Social Psychology. 2013;105: 301–315. doi: 10.1037/a0032278. pmid:23627748.

49. Carnes NC, Janoff-Bulman R. (in prep). Group Morality and the Function of Trust and Distrust.

50. Alford JR, Funk CL, Hibbing JR. Are political orientations genetically transmitted? American Political Science Review, 2005;99: 153–67.

51. Kron J. Red State, Blue City: How the Urban-Rural Divide Is Splitting America. The Atlantic, 30 Nov, 2012. Available: http://www.theatlantic.com/politics/archive/2012/11/red-state-blue-city-how-the-urban-rural-divide-is-splitting-america/265686/.

52. Wikipedia. List of Presidential election results by popular vote margin. 2014. Available: http://en.wikipedia.org/wiki/List_of_United_States_presidential_elections_by_popular_vote_margin.

53. Skitka LJ, Bauman CW, Sargis EG. Moral conviction: Another contributor to attitude strength or something more? Journal of Personality and Social Psychology. 2005;88: 895–917.

54. Parker MT, Janoff-Bulman R. Lessons from morality-based social identity: The power of outgroup "hate," not just ingroup "love." Social Justice Research. 2013;26: 81–96.

CHAPTER 3: WHAT THE COURTS SAY

EXCERPT FROM *BOY SCOUTS OF AMERICA ET AL. V. DALE*, 530 U.S. 640 (2000) FROM THE UNITED STATES SUPREME COURT

1. The record evidence sheds doubt on Dale's assertion. For example, the National Director of the Boy Scouts certified that "*any* persons who advocate to Scouting youth that homosexual conduct is" consistent with Scouting values will not be registered as adult leaders. App. 746 (emphasis added). And the Monmouth Council Scout Executive testified that the advocacy of the morality of homosexuality to youth members by any adult member is grounds for revocation of the adult's membership. *Id.*, at 761.

2. Public accommodations laws have also broadened in scope to cover more groups; they have expanded beyond those groups that have been given heightened equal protection scrutiny under our cases. See *Romer,* 517 U. S., at 629. Some municipal ordinances have even expanded to cover criteria such as prior criminal record, prior psychiatric treatment, military status, personal appearance, source of income, place of residence, and political ideology. See 1 Boston, Mass., Ordinance No. § 12-9.7 (1999) (ex-offender, prior psychiatric treatment, and military status); D. C. Code Ann. § 1-2519 (1999) (personal appearance, source of income, place of residence); Seattle, Wash., Municipal Code § 14.08.090 (1999) (political ideology).

3. Four State Supreme Courts and one United States Court of Appeals have ruled that the Boy Scouts is not a place of public accommodation. *Welsh* v. *Boy Scouts of America,* 993 F.2d 1267 *(CA7)*, cert. denied, 510 U. S. 1012 (1993); *Curran* v. *Mount Diablo Council of the Boy Scouts of America,* 17 Cal. 4th 670, 952 P. 2d 218 (1998); *Seabourn* v. *Coronado Area Council, Boy Scouts of America,* 257 Kan. 178, 891 P. 2d 385 (1995); *Quinnipiac Council, Boy Scouts of America, Inc.* v. *Comm'n on Human Rights & Opportunities,* 204

Conn. 287, 528 A. 2d 352 (1987); *Schwenk* v. *Boy Scouts of America*, 275 Ore. 327, 551 P. 2d 465 (1976). No federal appellate court or state supreme court-except the New Jersey Supreme Court in this case-has reached a contrary result.

4. We anticipated this result in *Hurley* when we illustrated the reasons for our holding in that case by likening the parade to a private membership organization. 515 U. S., at 580. We stated: "Assuming the parade to be large enough and a source of benefits (apart from its expression) that would generally justify a mandated access provision, GLIB could nonetheless be refused admission as an expressive contingent with its own message just as readily as a private club could exclude an applicant whose manifest views were at odds with a position taken by the club's existing members." *Id.*, at 580-581.

EXCERPT FROM *UNITED STATES V. VIRGINIA ET AL., 518 U.S. 515 (1996),* FROM THE UNITED STATES SUPREME COURT

5. As Thomas Jefferson stated the view prevailing when the Constitution was new:

"Were our State a pure democracy ... there would yet be excluded from their deliberations ... [w]omen, who, to prevent depravation of morals and ambiguity of issue, could not mix promiscuously in the public meetings of men." Letter from Thomas Jefferson to Samuel Kercheval (Sept. 5, 1816), in 10 Writings of Thomas Jefferson 45-46, n. 1 (P. Ford ed. 1899).

6. The Court has thus far reserved most stringent judicial scrutiny for classifications based on race or national origin, but last Term observed that strict scrutiny of such classifications is not inevitably "fatal in fact." *Adarand Constructors, Inc.* v. *Pena*, 515 U. S. 200, 237 (1995) (internal quotation marks omitted).

7. Several *amici* have urged that diversity in educational opportunities is an altogether appropriate governmental pursuit and that single-sex schools can contribute importantly to such diversity. Indeed, it is the mission of some single-sex schools "to dissipate, rather than perpetuate, traditional gender classifications." See Brief for Twenty-six Private Women's Colleges as *Amici Curiae* 5. We do not question the Commonwealth's

prerogative evenhandedly to support diverse educational opportunities. We address specifically and only an educational opportunity recognized by the District Court and the Court of Appeals as "unique," see 766 F. Supp., at 1413, 1432; 976 F. 2d, at 892, an opportunity available only at Virginia's premier military institute, the Commonwealth's sole single-sex public university or college. Cf. *Mississippi Univ. for Women* v. *Hogan*, 458 U. S. 718, 720, n. 1 (1982) ("Mississippi maintains no other single-sex public university or college. Thus, we are not faced with the question of whether States can provide 'separate but equal' undergraduate institutions for males and females.").

8. On this point, the dissent sees fire where there is no flame. See *post,* at 596-598, 598-600. "Both men and women can benefit from a single-sex education," the District Court recognized, although "the beneficial effects" of such education, the court added, apparently "are stronger among women than among men." 766 F. Supp., at 1414. The United States does not challenge that recognition. Cf. C. Jencks & D. Riesman, The Academic Revolution 297-298 (1968):

   > "The pluralistic argument for preserving all-male colleges is uncomfortably similar to the pluralistic argument for preserving all-white colleges .... The all-male college would be relatively easy to defend if it emerged from a world in which women were established as fully equal to men. But it does not. It is therefore likely to be a witting or unwitting device for preserving tacit assumptions of male superiority-assumptions for which women must eventually pay."

9. Dr. Edward H. Clarke of Harvard Medical School, whose influential book, Sex in Education, went through 17 editions, was perhaps the most well-known speaker from the medical community opposing higher education for women. He maintained that the physiological effects of hard study and academic competition with boys would interfere with the development of girls' reproductive organs. See E. Clarke, Sex in Education 38-39, 62-63 (1873); *id.,* at 127 ("identical education of the two sexes is a crime before God and humanity, that physiology protests against, and that experience weeps over"); see also H. Maudsley, Sex in Mind and in Education 17 (1874) ("It is not that girls have not ambition, nor that they fail generally to run the intellectual race [in coeducational settings], but it is asserted that they do it at a cost to their strength and health which entails life-long suffering,

and even incapacitates them for the adequate performance of the natural functions of their sex."); C. Meigs, Females and Their Diseases 350 (1848) (after five or six weeks of "mental and educational discipline," a healthy woman would "lose ... the habit of menstruation" and suffer numerous ills as a result of depriving her body for the sake of her mind).

10. Virginia's Superintendent of Public Instruction dismissed the coeducational idea as '"repugnant to the prejudices of the people'" and proposed a female college similar in quality to Girton, Smith, or Vassar. 2 History of Women's Education 254 (quoting Dept. of Interior, 1 Report of Commissioner of Education, H. R. Doc. No.5, 58th Cong., 2d Sess., 438 (1904)).

11. See *post,* at 566, 598-599, 603. Forecasts of the same kind were made regarding admission of women to the federal military academies. See, *e. g.*, Hearings on H. R. 9832 et al. before Subcommittee No.2 of the House Committee on Armed Services, 93d Cong., 2d Sess., 137 (1975) (statement of Lt. Gen. A. P. Clark, Superintendent of U. S. Air Force Academy) ("It is my considered judgment that the introduction of female cadets will inevitably erode this vital atmosphere."); *id.*, at 165 (statement of Hon. H. H. Callaway, Secretary of the Army) ("Admitting women to West Point would irrevocably change the Academy .... The Spartan atmospherewhich is so important to producing the final product-would surely be diluted, and would in all probability disappear.").

12 See 766 F. Supp., at 1413 (describing testimony of expert witness David Riesman: "[I]f VMI were to admit women, it would eventually find it necessary to drop the adversative system altogether, and adopt a system that provides more nurturing and support for the students."). Such judgments have attended, and impeded, women's progress toward full citizenship stature throughout our Nation's history. Speaking in 1879 in support of higher education for females, for example, Virginia State Senator C. T. Smith of Nelson recounted that legislation proposed to pro tect the property rights of women had encountered resistance. 10 Educ. J. Va. 213 (1879). A Senator opposing the measures objected that "there [was] no formal call for the [legislation]," and "depicted in burning eloquence the terrible consequences such laws would produce." *Ibid.* The legislation passed, and a year or so later, its sponsor, C. T. Smith, reported

that "not one of [the forecast "terrible consequences"] has or ever will happen, even unto the sounding of Gabriel's trumpet." *Ibid.* See also *supra,* at 537-538.

13. Women cadets have graduated at the top of their class at every federal military academy. See Brief for Lieutenant Colonel Rhonda Cornum et al. as *Amici Curiae* 11, n. 25; cf. Defense Advisory Committee on Women in the Services, Report on the Integration and Performance of Women at West Point 64 (1992).

14. Brief for Lieutenant Colonel Rhonda Cornum, *supra,* at 5-9 (reporting the vital contributions and courageous performance of women in the military); see Mintz, President Nominates 1st Woman to Rank of Three-Star General, Washington Post, Mar. 27, 1996, p. A19, col. 1 (announcing President's nomination of Marine Corps Major General Carol Mutter to rank of Lieutenant General; Mutter will head corps manpower and planning); Tousignant, A New Era for the Old Guard, Washington Post, Mar. 23, 1996, p. *C1,* col. 2 (reporting admission of Sergeant Heather Johnsen to elite Infantry unit that keeps round-the-clock vigil at Tomb of the Unknowns in Arlington National Cemetery).

15. Inclusion of women in settings where, traditionally, they were not wanted inevitably entails a period of adjustment. As one West Point cadet squad leader recounted: "[T]he classes of '78 and '79 see the women as women, but the classes of '80 and '81 see them as classmates." U. S. Military Academy, A. Vitters, Report of Admission of Women (Project Athena II) 84 (1978) (internal quotation marks omitted).

16. VMI has successfully managed another notable change. The school admitted its first African-American cadets in 1968. See The VMI Story 347-349 (students no longer sing "Dixie," salute the Confederate flag or the tomb of General Robert E. Lee at ceremonies and sports events). As the District Court noted, VMI established a program on "retention of black cadets" designed to offer academic and social-cultural support to "minority members of a dominantly white and tradition-oriented student body." 766 F. Supp., at 1436-1437. The school maintains a "special recruitment program for blacks" which, the District Court found, "has had little, if any, effect on VMI's method of accomplishing its mission." *Id.*, at 1437.

GLOSSARY

apartheid—A policy of segregation and discrimination against black Africans that was in place in South Africa from 1948 until 1992.

Black Lives Matter—A social justice movement that arose after the killings of unarmed black men by police in 2014 and 2015.

capitalism—An economic system in which businesses are controlled by private owners and not the government.

climate change—The idea that the planet is undergoing a drastic change in climate and that the changes are caused in part by human actions.

food desert—A community in which it is difficult to find affordable fresh foods, such as fruits and vegetables; often found in rural and urban areas, but rarely in the suburbs. Poor and marginalized communities frequently live in food deserts.

homosexual—A person who is attracted to members of the same sex; gay men and lesbians are homosexual.

income gap—The difference between the poorest and the wealthiest members of a society; also called a "wealth gap."

marginalized—A person or group that is oppressed or vulnerable by a majority class.

morality—To have morals, or to behave in a way that is deemed moral, or correct; not following the rules, necessarily, but doing what is best for people.

politically correct—Something that is nondiscriminatory or neutral; often used in a negative fashion when discussing social justice.

poverty—Extremely poor. In the US, a person is in poverty if they make less than $11,880 per year, or if their family makes less than $16,020.

privatization—When a service typically provided by a public group, such as the government, is taken over by a privately owned business.

race—Often used interchangeably with "ethnicity"; a group of people that shares similar physical characteristics, often broken down by skin color.

social justice—Equality in terms of the distribution of wealth, access to opportunities, and wealth.

suffrage—The right to vote.

FOR MORE INFORMATION

BOOKS

Coates, Ta-Nehisi. *Between the World and Me.* New York, NY: Spiegel & Grau, 2015.

Linker, Maureen. *Intellectual Empathy: Critical Thinking for Social Justice.* Ann Arbor, MI: University of Michigan Press, 2015.

Novak, Michael and Paul Adams with Elizabeth Shaw. *Social Justice Isn't What You Think It Is.* New York, NY: Encounter Books, 2015.

Schatz, Kate. *Rad American Woman A – Z.* San Francisco, CA: City Lights Books, 2015.

Sensoy, Özlem and Robin DiAngelo. *Is Everyone Really Equal? An Introduction to Key Concepts in Social Justice Education*. New York, NY: Teachers College Press, 2012.

Vance, J. D. *Hillbilly Elegy: A Memoir of a Family and Culture in Crisis*. New York, NY: HarperCollins, 2016.

WEBSITES

American Civil Liberties Union (ACLU)

www.aclu.org

The ACLU works to fight for the rights of marginalized and oppressed classes of people in the United States. The organization, founded nearly one hundred years ago, uses the legal system in order to help vulnerable citizens. The group focuses primarily on the rights guaranteed to citizens by the Constitution, and works to ensure that all citizens have equal rights under the law.

National Association for the Advancement of Colored People (NAACP)

www.naacp.org

Founded in 1909, the NAACP works to help black citizens achieve political, educational, social, and economic equality. They also work hard to fight against race-based discrimination. Members of the NAACP were involved in the work that lead to the reversal of the *Plessy v. Ferguson* decision by the US Supreme Court and ended the segregation of public schools in America.

National Organization for Women (NOW)

www.now.org

The National Organization for Women, founded in 1966, in the midst of the original feminist movement, works to achieve equality for all women in all areas of their lives, from the workplace and the classroom to the voting booth and the public street. NOW members have achieved such accomplishments as being the first black woman elected to the US Congress (Shirley Chisholm), as well as fighting to get *Roe v. Wade* decided in the Supreme Court, and drafting the Equal Rights Amendment.

INDEX

A

African National Congress, 36–40
Alfaro, Carlos, 133
Allen, Myles R., 165
apartheid, 36–40
Aristotle, virtue ethics of, 178

B

Barbosa, Lívia, 182–198
Bauer, Peter, 8–9
Black History Month, 154–156
Black Lives Matter, 4, 53–54, 157–160, 201
blind jurors, 128–130
Blumenauer, Earl, 145
Board of Directors of Rotary Int'l v. Rotary Club of Duarte, 68–69, 81, 82
Boyer, David, 138
Boy Scouts of America et al. v. Dale, 66–85
Bryant, Jeff, 199–204
Burley, Jamira, 160

C

Campbell, Katie, 133–145
Capital in the Twenty-First Century, 7, 41
Carnes, Nate C., 15–27
Castile, Philando, 158
charity, as key to fighting poverty, 49–52
China, 9–10
climate change, 6, 32–35, 163–166
Clinton, Hillary Rodham, 46, 55–63
Coalition for a Drug-Free Hawaii, 135
Cohen, Richard, 171
Collins, William A., 174
Common Dreams, 158
Correia, Michael, 143, 144

D

Dace, Paul, 179
Dale, James, 66–85
Daniel, Kent D., 166
Daniels, Mitch, 13–14
Dasgupta, Rana, 42, 44
Dash, Stacey, 156
deaf people
    as jurors, 128–130
    and the police, 146–150
Deng Xiaoping, 9–10
deontological ethics, 178
Diniz, Debora, 182–198
disabilities, 182–198
Dorn, James A., 7–10
Drug Enforcement Administration, 135
Drug Policy Alliance, 135, 136
Duffin, Kevin, 168

E

Edelman, Marian Wright, 151–153

F

food assistance programs, privatization and, 13
food deserts, 151–153
Ford, Gerald, 155
Frayling, Timothy, 28–31, 213
Fulton, Deidre, 157–160

G

Gardner, Cooper, 53–54
Garza, Alicia, 159
Global Agricultural Alliance, 34
Greco, Emily Schwartz, 172–174
Green, Kathryn, 6, 32–35
Green Climate Fund, 33
Greenstone, Michael, 166
Gurciullo, Brianna, 133–145

H

Hagopian, Jesse, 200, 201, 203, 204
Harkins, Steven, 176–179
hate crimes, 167–171
height and inequality, 28–31
Hurley v. Irish American Gay, Lesbian and Bisexual Group of Boston, 69, 70, 71, 77, 80, 81, 83

I

individual responsibility, as key to fighting poverty, 49–52
inequality, 6, 7–10, 28–31, 41–44, 132, 162
    disabled people and, 182–198
    height and weight and, 28–31
    and the media, 172–174
    and privatization, 11–14

J

Jacobs, James, 169
Jaffe, Sarah, 204
Janoff-Bulman, Ronnie, 15–27
Jeffery, Anthea, 38
Johnson, Ron, 49–52
Joseph Project, 50
JUSTISIGNS project, 148–150

K
Kaepernick, Colin, 206–207, 212
Kampia, Rob, 136–137
Kant, Immanuel, 178
Kennedy, Sheila, 11–14
King, Martin Luther, Jr., 36–40
King, Shaun, 48, 49
Knight, Nika, 47–49
Kurdi, Aylan, 176
Kurtenbach, Mike, 53

L
Lazarus, Richard J., 166
Legalize Maine, 138–139
Levin, Brian, 170
Lewis, Peter, 136
Litterman, Robert B., 166
Lynch, Loretta, 54
Lyons, Gaye, 128

M
Mahoney, Brendan, 48
Malthus, Thomas, 177
Mandela, Nelson, 36, 37
Mao Zedong, 9
marijuana legalization, 133–145
Marijuana Policy Project, 133, 134, 136, 137, 138, 139, 144
Marikana tragedy, 43
Markham, Claire, 49–52
Marx, Karl, 41, 44
Matthee, Keith, 6, 36–40
Mawdsley, Karen, 133–145
McCarrier, Paul, 139
Mckesson, DeRay, 158
media, lack of diversity in, 172–174
Medicaid, privatization and, 13
Mezzadri, Alessandra, 41–44
morality, 15–27
Morial, Marc, 154–156
Muslim ban, 208–211

N
Napier, Jemina, 128–130, 146–150, 213
National Organization for the Reform of Marijuana Laws (NORML), 134, 136, 137, 142
National Urban League Equality Index, 156
Native Americans, 4
New Climate Economy, 34
nutrition, as matter of social justice, 151–153

O
Obama, Barack, 142, 143, 163, 202
Obama, Michelle, 153
Op-Ed Project, 173

P
Paul, Rand, 134
PC culture, 5
Peña-Rodriguez v. Colorado, 119–126
Piketty, Thomas, 7, 41, 43, 44
Piper, Bill, 135
Plessy v. Ferguson, 102–118
privatization and inequality, 11–14
Prupis, Nadia, 206–207
Pyle, Thomas, 164

Q
Quindlen, Anna, 172

R
refugees, 4, 176–179
Respect State Marijuana Laws Act, 145
Revkin, Andrew, 163–166
Rifai, Dina el-, 208–211
Riffle, Dan, 144, 145
Rights and Resources Initiative, 34
Roberts, David, 166
Roberts v. United States Jaycees, 70, 73, 81, 82
Rohrabacher, Dana, 145
Rufino dos Santos, Wederson, 182–198
Ryan, Paul, 49–52, 132

S
Schumpeter, Joseph, 8
Sexton, Joe, 167–171
Shinn, Alan, 135
social justice education, 46, 47–49
Soros, George, 136
South Africa, 36–40, 43, 58
Southern Poverty Law Center, 171
Stanton, Greg, 53, 54
Sterling, Alton, 158
St. Pierre, Allen, 137
Stroup, Keith, 134, 140, 141, 142
Sunstein, Cass R., 166

T
Thatcher, Margaret, 12
Third Way, 141
Thorpe, Bob, 47
Tometi, Opal, 160
Trumble, Sarah, 141, 142
Trump, Donald, 163, 164, 167, 169, 208–211
Tuchman, Gaye, 179

Tvert, Mason, 136, 137, 138, 140
Tyrrell, Jessica, 28–31, 213

U
United States v. Virginia et al., 86–102
Utilitarianism, 178

V
violence, 6, 36–40
Virginia Military Institute, 86–102
Voices from the Climate Front Lines, 33

W
Wagner, Gernot, 164, 166
Walton, Reginald, 53, 54
weight and inequality, 28–31
women's rights, 46, 55–63
Woodson, Carter G., 154–155
World Economic Forum 2015, 43
World Resources Institute, 34

Z
Zepeda, Mario Moreno, 143

ABOUT THE EDITOR

Jennifer Peters is a writer and editor whose work has focused on everything from relationships to books to military and defense issues. During her more than ten years working in the media, her work has appeared in a number of magazines and online news and culture sites, with her most recent bylines appearing on *VICE News* and *Task & Purpose*. She lives in New York City, and she never leaves home without a good book.